Encountering Burges:

Reflections on the Art and Architecture of the
Chapel at Worcester College, Oxford

Encountering Burges:

Reflections on the Art and Architecture of the
Chapel at Worcester College, Oxford

Susan Gillingham

THIRD MILLENNIUM
PUBLISHING, LONDON

A note on the text:
Capital letters have been kept to a minimum, except for College-specific
terms, proper nouns, and sacred entities and language. All Bible excerpts
come from the New Revised Standard Version.

Excerpt from T.S. Eliot's 'Journey of the Magi' on p.64 © Eliot Literary
Estate and Faber & Faber

Encountering Burges: Reflections on the Art and
Architecture of the Chapel at Worcester College, Oxford
© Dr Susan Gillingham and Third Millennium Publishing Limited

First published in 2009 by
Third Millennium Publishing Limited,
a subsidiary of Third Millennium Information Limited.

2–5 Benjamin Street
London
United Kingdom
EC1M 5QL
www.tmiltd.com

ISBN: 978 1 906507 47 3

British Library Cataloguing in Publication Data
A CIP catalogue record for this book is available from the British Library.

Written by Susan Gillingham
Designed by Matthew Wilson
Production by Bonnie Murray

Reprographics by Asia Graphics, HK
Printed by Henry Ling, UK

Contents

Preface

For enabling the production of this book I must first thank three chaplains of Worcester College, who, in their different ways, encouraged the preaching of these nine sermons on the seven windows and two canticles. The Revd Canon Dr Peter Doll (1998–2002) was the first, and his interest in church history, liturgy and architecture was invaluable in getting the project under way. The Revd Emma Pennington (2003–08) was the second, and she gave me the challenge of fitting the sermons, which each had its own theme, into different themes of the sermon series which she had selected for the whole term. Most of the sermons were given during her time at Worcester, and Emma's support, good humour and friendship have been invaluable. The Revd Dr Jonathan Arnold (2008–) came in at the end of the project, but nevertheless warmly encouraged me to preach the two remaining sermons. All three chaplains are gifted musicians, and to preach in the context of the anthems they helped to choose, with the various chapel choirs they have encouraged, has always been an inspiration.

I also owe several other colleagues in the College my gratitude for their support. Above all is Dr Joanna Parker, our Librarian, who allowed me to free access to Wyatt's and Burges' designs and plans kept in the College Library; she always tried to answer the most inane and odd questions about the history of the period of the Chapel's refurbishment (she may remember how the two Daniel brothers initially gave much confusion) and has been gracious in every way. She also pointed me in the direction of several literary resources, including the Daniel collection in the library (Daniel MS 12), and these have given the introduction a better focus. Ms Vanda Thomas, Secretary to the Estates Bursar, was helpful in chasing up valuable visual material from the period of the Chapel's memorable facelift in 2002 from Cliveden Conservation Workshop, Taplow; Cliveden were most generous in giving me CDs of their many images from the time of the Chapel's restoration – they were able to capture the Chapel's art and architecture at angles which have been impossible since the scaffolding came down, and I have used many of

Dr Susan Gillingham is Fellow and Tutor in Theology at Worcester College, Reader in Old Testament at Oxford University, and licensed Lay Minister in the Diocese of Oxford.

them here. The photograph of Burges (a distinctive image, from his family collection, *right*) and of the Summer Smoking Room in Cardiff Castle were given by kind permission of Matthew Williams, Curator of Cardiff Castle; the staff there were particularly helpful. I am grateful to Ms Coleen Day, the College's Director of Development, who provided me with important resources from previous issues of the *Worcester College Magazine*, as well as a useful database of old members who might be interested in purchasing this publication.

Although any errors in the text are my responsibility alone, I am nevertheless indebted to a number of people who read the text and who commented on it from different viewpoints. Dr Jonathan Arnold was typically thorough and helpful; so too was Dr Joanna Parker. Dr Natasha O'Hear, a Junior Research Fellow in Theology at Worcester and for three years my research assistant, read the text with an eye to visual exegesis; she was also invaluable in helping with the selection of relevant images. My husband, Dick Smethurst, with his somewhat disconcerting eye for precision, read the text at least twice and his extraordinary detailed knowledge of the College's history prevented some embarrassing errors. As always, I am indebted to his constant love and support.

The images have come from a variety of sources. I have acknowledged the external sources above. My daughter, Abbie, took some four hundred shots of the Chapel's art and architecture; I was constantly relieved that no one entered the Chapel when she was lying on her back on the floor or clambering on the backs of the pews to get a relevant image. These provided the basis of the first draft, and many of those images have been used in the final version. But I also needed a large number of professional images. Mr Keith Barnes, of Photographers Workshop, Oxford, with whom I have worked previously on Faculty publications, was an obvious choice, and although the vicissitudes of the late summer sun caused us some frustration and amusement, Keith's enjoyment of natural light and shade resulted in most of these images being taken without artificial illumination; I think even Burges might have been pleased with the final effect.

From an aesthetic point of view, I really owe the final form to Matt Wilson, the Art Director at Third Millennium Publishing, who transformed my draft into what it is now, without fuss and always with attention to detail. Ms Bonnie Murray, the Publishing Manager at Third Millennium has kept the schedule on time. Finally, Christopher Fagg, the Publisher at Third Millennium, deserves special thanks, not only because of his willingness to take on this somewhat unusual project in the first place and but also because of his unflappable support throughout.

The project has been a great exercise in teamwork, and for those mentioned above and others who have contributed in less obvious ways, I am most grateful.

Introduction

This is not another history of Worcester Chapel. I am not a church historian, and my academic competence in matters historical ends at the point when the history of the Christian church begins. Nor is it a visitor's guide to the architecture of the chapel; I am certainly not an art historian, and my interest in William Burges' nineteenth-century refurbishment of the chapel is more theological than aesthetic. This book is a collection of nine sermons, originally given over a period of some six years at specific occasions in the life of the chapel; each was composed around a visual feature of the chapel: seven windows and two inscriptions. I have prefaced them with this extended introduction which is intended to help the reader understand better the purpose and contents of the sermons themselves.

This introduction is in three parts. The first is a selective history of the chapel, focusing especially on its Benedictine foundations. The sermons have several references to the Rule of Benedict, and a recurring theme is the importance of Benedictine spirituality. Hence the fact that the chapel was founded by the 'Black Monks', with their liturgical space continuing in one form or another on much the same site for some seven hundred years, has been an important inspiration for the preparation and delivery of the addresses. The second part of the introduction focuses on the nineteenth-century iconography of the chapel: its purpose is to try to understand the influences upon Burges' often overwhelming designs, for there is so much hidden as well as explicit in what has been expressed on the walls, windows, ceiling and floor of the chapel. Because each of the sermons interprets various aspects of the chapel's architecture theologically, usually constrained by a specific liturgical occasion, something more general on the chapel's architecture should help readers understand better the more precise allusions to the iconography in the sermons. The third part is a brief account of my theological method: I have called this 'visual exegesis', because it is about a written (or spoken) interpretation of visual representations of biblical texts and themes. This is of course easier to appreciate when you are surrounded by the actual iconography in the chapel; because the medium was originally the spoken word, reproducing it in a written form inevitably loses vitality and immediacy. So in this part of this introduction I will seek to make explicit what in the delivery of the sermons was more intuitive and implicit.

The Benedictine Foundations

For anyone interested in the early impact of Benedictine theology, the pre-history of Worcester College – the period when it was known as Gloucester College (1283–1541) – offers an excellent example, because this site accommodated the very first Benedictine 'house of study' at Oxford.[1] The earliest records about founding a community for intellectually able Benedictine monks are in the statutes of the General Chapter of the Benedictine Province of Canterbury, held at Reading in 1277. The increasingly pervasive influence of university education, the success of Dominican, Franciscan and Carmelite friars at Oxford, and the presence of yet other monastic communities – for example, the Cistercians at Rewley, the Augustinians at Osney and St Frideswide's Priory – together impelled the Benedictine Chapter to consider a university education for their own monks.

---

[1] See, for example, A. Léotard OSB and R.G.M. McHardy (1997), pp. 20–36; also J. Campbell, (1997), pp. 37–47.

Fig.1: Each of the Cottages still preserves the arms of their monastic community. Inset: the red griffin of the Benedictines of Malmesbury Abbey.

Six years later, the annals of Gloucester Abbey record the presence in Oxford of Benedictines from that house, acknowledging that this was due to the generosity of 'the noble Sir John Giffard'.[2] John Giffard of Brimpsfield was a wealthy baron with royal connections and several properties in the Cotswolds, and he had acquired from the Hospitallers of St John the mansion of Gilbert of Clare which was in Stockwell Street, opposite the 'royal palace' (later, Beaumont Palace) and close to the Carmelite monastery. He gave this site, at least initially, to be used as a 'house of study' by the Benedictines of St Peter's Abbey, Gloucester. Further insights into these early initiatives are found in a letter written in April of the same year (1283) by Godfrey Giffard, Bishop of Worcester (cousin of John Giffard) to the 'Chancellor and University of Oxford', requesting that the Black Monks should be given a 'doctor of the divine page' (a DD) 'that the way of learning may lie open to those thirsting for wisdom, and so at least, they themselves becoming learned, may be able to instruct the people to the honour of God and the Church.'[3]

Until 1291 the venture comprised a cell of some thirteen monks, all from St Peter's Abbey. Then John Giffard provided for four other tenements; the Benedictine chapter responded by decreeing that the site should now become an independent priory, although each monastic community was to be responsible for the upkeep of its own buildings. The first prior was Henry de Helliun of Gloucester

---

[2] See A. Léotard OSB and R.G.M. McHardy (1997) p. 21, and notes 11 and 12.

[3] The document has been preserved at Worcester County Library, MS. BA26 48/1 (i), folio 205 (ccvi). See A. Léotard OSB and R.G.M. McHardy (1997), p. 21 and note 9.

Abbey. Also in 1291, Osney Abbey – under whose auspices the newly formed priory fell – recorded that 'the monks of St Benedict in Stockwell Street' should be exempt the requisite tithe of 6s. 8d. a year, and that they should be free to build their own chapel with the right of their own cemetery. The main obstacle to this agreement was, predictably, financial, exacerbated by the diffuse nature of the community with its diverse monastic cells. The chapel was actually not built until the 1420s.[4]

By 1298 the Benedictine Order finally recognised this *studium generale* (by then augmented by monks from other abbeys and monasteries from the Province of Canterbury) as 'Gloucester College'. The title was in fact a misnomer – despite the oversight of a single prior, this was a religious institution of individual monastic cells and it was certainly not a collegiate community: the title 'Hall' (one which was actually used for the period between 1560 and 1714) would have been more appropriate. A further misnomer was that Gloucester Abbey was no longer the owner of the site, Giffard having transferred that privilege to the Benedictines of Malmesbury Abbey (Fig.1). But the name Gloucester College stuck. In 1298, one William de Broc of Gloucester was the first monk to gain a university degree: admittedly this was not a DD, but a Bachelor of Theology, yet the event was still apparently marked with great festivity. William had earned his degree by spending three years on the study of the Bible and at least a further two on 'Disputations, Responsions and Determinations'.[5]

We know very little of the liturgical life of Gloucester College during this early period, partly because work on the chapel did not begin until so much later. Given that the Benedictine presence in Oxford was primarily for academic purposes, we have little evidence about whether, for example, the different cells worshipped together or in their separate *camerae*, sharing resources only with others who were less well endowed. After 1320, the Carmelites moved eastwards across Stockwell Street into 'Beaumont Palace' (a property given to them by Edward II in 1314). This enabled the Benedictine Order to purchase the Carmelite Friary for their own use, and it seems likely that William de Camme, the then Prior of Gloucester College, would have made full use of the former Carmelite chapel at least for festal occasions.

What was taking place at Gloucester College between the end of the thirteenth century and beginning of the fourteenth was in fact typical of many other monastic communities. What made Gloucester College distinctive (along with Durham [later Trinity] College, founded in 1291) was its Benedictine foundation; and what made it peculiar, even when compared with Durham College, which provided for monks from the Province of York, was its ongoing disparate nature because of its independent monastic units. Although Gloucester College possessed a large extent of land (which was essentially water meadow, rather like Port Meadow today) this did not stimulate the same rapid growth on its site as the better endowed colleges of Balliol, University, Merton and Exeter were undergoing. Merton, for example, founded in 1264, was by the beginning of the fourteenth century already well equipped with a quadrangle, treasury, library, and chapel quire.

---

[4] By contrast, Durham College, for example, had a more secure endowment, and although it only professed some six to ten monks until the end of the fourteenth century, by 1326 it possessed a licence for an oratory and permission to build a chapel. (Ironically, as at Gloucester College, these were not completed until the beginning of the fifteenth century.)

[5] A DD, compared with a Bachelor of Theology degree, would have taken some seventeen years – eight years mainly in logic and philosophy, and nine years in theology.

Another milestone was between 1336 and 1338, when Pope Benedict XII made it compulsory that 'one in twenty' monks from each of the Benedictine houses – from York as well as Canterbury – should undergo university study. Gloucester College thus grew in numbers as well as status. Durham College continued to take Benedictine monks from the northern province; Gloucester, those from the south.[6] This expansion exposed even more the need for a common library and chapel. It seems a small chapel had by this time been created on the actual site by converting a couple of rooms on the site of the present Hall; these were inadequate for the expanding community, but any creation of an adequate larger liturgical space was always constrained by lack of finances.

We know about the debates over the necessary expansion because of the accounts in the records of those individual abbeys who had *camerae* at Gloucester College. St Albans is an important resource in this respect, and its abbots contributed quite generously to the building fund. For example, Thomas de la Mare, who used his period as President of the Benedictine Chapter in 1363 to publish statutes concerning a more regularised formation of the students at Oxford, persuaded the Abbey of St Albans to enable the reparation of some of the furnishings and houses, and to set up a fund for a new chapel. By 1401 Abbot Heyworth, also from St Albans, had brought some of these building projects to completion. But it was not until 1420 – nearly a hundred and thirty years after the first monastic cell had been established on the site – that the building of the new chapel began in earnest, using the funds for this purpose which had been started during the time of Abbot de la Mare. John Whethamsted, another Abbot of St Albans, was an influential donor and, as one of the first 'elected' Priors of Gloucester College, it seems he was most committed to its advancement. Not only did he give generously to the chapel, but he was also responsible for the building of a library to the south of the chapel, giving many of his own books – including an assortment of tracts against Lollardy, still preserved today – to the collection.

Whethamsted's chapel was completed in about 1424. What few records we have inform us that the chapel had stained-glass windows of the Crucifixion, the Virgin Mary and John the Baptist (its patron saint, with Benedict), as well as representations of saints, monks and bishops, as well as various inscriptions. We know from a 1675 drawing by Loggan (to be discussed in detail below) that this was partly on the site on which the chapel stands today, and along with the library and the dining hall (which was built on the south west side of the chapel, also partly on the present site) the three buildings at last provided visibly for that corporate life in the Benedictine tradition which was represented by prayer, study and manual work.[7] It is interesting to see how – albeit not for the same theological reasons – the present design around the cloisters gives us some continuity with our Benedictine forbears.[8]

---

[6] Some of these parent houses are still visible today through the arms above the staircase doors to the various *camerae*, for example those on staircases 9 (perhaps belonging to Pershore Abbey), 10 (the cross and virgin indicating Glastonbury Abbey), 11 (with the cross of St Augustine's, Canterbury) and 12 (with the griffin of Malmesbury Abbey). Less visible are other *camerae* to the north (St Alban's Abbey, roughly on the site of staircase 4, and, on the site of the present SCR, at one time Bury St Edmund's) and to the south, where the Pump Quad is now (which was probably the original *camera* of Glastonbury).

[7] For example, *Rule of Benedict XLVIII* divides the day up into Prayer (the *Opus Dei*, or Divine Office), Manual Labour (*Ora*) and Study (*Lectio Divina*). Given the central place of these three aspects of monastic life in the Benedictine Rule, it is hard to think that the close locations of the chapel, library and refectory were an accident. Durham College, too, mirrored these relationships in its architecture.

[8] The sermons on pp.43–109 appeal on more than one occasion to the same triad of prayer, academic study and labour and show how this may be mirrored in the interconnection of Chapel, Library and Hall.

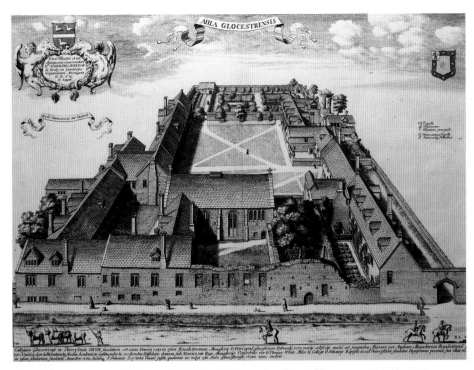

Fig.2: Original engraving of Gloucester Hall by David Loggan from Oxonia Illustrata, *published in 1675.*

Whethamsted's long-awaited chapel survived for just over a century. By 1541, the whole monastic community had been possessed by the king – ironically precisely because the diverse cells had never agreed on being incorporated into a single academic establishment. A property survey dating from 1559 informs us that the chapel had disappeared and the land upon which it had stood was now 'to be rented yearelie…'.[9] In 1567, seven years after Sir Thomas White (a wealthy merchant and founder of St John's College) had bought the entire site, William Stock was appointed Principal of what was now to be called Gloucester Hall (initially operating under the auspices of St John's). We know that the library, too, had been ruined, for the records reveal that it was now used as a 'garnett or place for the College to lay their corn'.[10] Gloucester Hall survived from 1560 to 1714. A later print by David Loggan (Fig.2), originally dated about 1675, gives us further insights about the rebuilding of the chapel, hall and library by the latter part of the seventeenth century. Loggan's is the earliest extant drawing which illustrates the layout in any detail: in the engraving above we can see the earlier position of John Whethamstede's (still-ruined) chapel, with an east door curiously opening out on to the street, and the partly ruined former library, on the first floor of what was known as the Bury building (which before 1540 had included a large *camera* on the ground floor); the library's nine windows also opened onto the street.

Loggan's engraving not only illustrates the locations of the first chapel and library during its period as Gloucester College, but also shows the positioning of the chapel, library and refectory as part of Gloucester Hall. The new chapel – discernible by the cross on the roof on the north side – is set almost in the middle of the present cloisters, and the hall (probably replacing a hall on the same site) adjoins it to the south. The library is partly on the site of the older Bury building. The late fourteenth and early

---

[9]   See R.A. Devereux and D.N. Griffiths (1951, revised edition 1994), p. 7.

[10]   *Ibid,* p. 10.

Fig.3: Today's Chapel (left), Library (centre) and Dining Hall (right), viewed across the main quadrangle.

fifteenth centuries had marked a time of financial support and new corporate buildings for Gloucester College; the early seventeenth century marked the same for Gloucester Hall, especially after it had gained self-governance (independent of St John's College, which still held the freehold) in 1626.

The chapel remained on this site throughout the last years of the Hall's history and survived for the first few years of the newly founded Worcester College. Hopes for any expansion ebbed and flowed throughout this time. One of the most interesting periods was during Benjamin Woodroffe's Principalship (1694–1711). That the chapel was one of his great concerns is evident in his high-profile clerical interests, including a brief Chaplaincy to Charles II, an even briefer period as Dean of Christ Church, and a lifelong preferment as Dean of Lichfield. Woodroffe's weakness was his somewhat reckless vision, for his plans for any refurbishment of the Chapel (and Dining Hall and Library) went far beyond his and the Hall's means: after a temporary experiment with a 'Greek College' between 1694 and 1705 failed to mature, and after he had served time in 1706 in the Fleet Prison for debt, his plans for new building projects simply ground to a halt.[11]

When the legacy of yet another Worcestershire baronet, Sir Thomas Cookes, eventually settled on Gloucester Hall, with Principal Blechyndon becoming the first Provost of the newly founded Worcester College in 1714, the accrued sum of £15,000 was still insufficient to allow for any further development,

---

[11] For a brief but useful account of the re-founding of the Chapel, see C.H. Daniel and W.R. Barker (1900). pp. 213–217.

Fig.4: Wyatt's design for the West Door with pilasters.

Fig.5: Wyatt's design for the walls.

for this could only cover the emoluments of the Provost and the Fellows and Scholars. It was not until 1720 that any new building projects could really begin, and even these were minimal, the result of a legacy of less than £1,000. But at least this was a period of innovative planning and designs. In preparation for actual building, the chapel was relocated to the south of its previous site (approximately to where the Junior Common Room is now). This was a 'temporary' move, but actually lasted for over seventy years, due, yet again, to shortage of funds impeding the progress of building. For reasons of respect for tradition rather than any emulation of Benedictine theology, the close relationship between the Chapel, Library and Dining Hall was always intended to continue (Fig.4). Dr George Clarke was initially responsible for the new designs (in consultation, it seems, with Hawksmoor). Clarke had a particular interest in the library as the place which would preserve his own and his father's collection, including the architectural drawings of Inigo Jones. The library was completed only after Clarke's death in 1736; this and the development of the terrace, including the structure of the chapel, were continued by Henry Keene. Upon his death in 1776, the final stages – the completion of interiors of the chapel and dining hall – were undertaken by an architect already employed by several Oxford colleges (the best known of his work is probably Peckwater Quadrangle at Christ Church), James Wyatt.[12]

So the chapel returned to its 1424 Benedictine location, and was duly consecrated in 1791. It was somewhat larger than its predecessor, although the records do not allow a detailed comparison between the interior of Wyatt's chapel and that of Whethamstede. Its austerity and simplicity certainly had some correspondences with Benedictine spirituality, but its *raison d'être* was clearly very different: Wyatt had also been the interior architect for Heveningham Hall, Suffolk (1778–80), and it is apparent that these designs influenced in no small way the understated approach to the chapel at Worcester: certainly the domed ceiling and the fans above the cornice echo the architecture there, causing some to call it 'an ecclesiastical drawing room'.[13] Wyatt worked on the chapel from 1776–91; his design drawings have been preserved in the library (Figs 4, 5 and 6). He modelled the chapel on a rectangular Neoclassical design, breaking up the space with quarter-

---

[12] Clarke had always intended to demolish all the medieval *camerae* lying to the north and south of the quadrangle, and replace them with classical wings on each side. Keene abandoned this plan, mainly for financial reasons, giving the main quadrangle its more lopsided appeal as viewed today.

[13] See D. Mordaunt Crook (1981), p. 146.

circle curves in each corner. Columns and pilasters were laid against the walls, and the simplicity – and, it could be argued, the austerity – of the walls, West Door and ceilings can be seen in his drawings represented here. The effect can be imagined by standing in the centre of the present Dining Hall, because its proportions (other than the dome which Wyatt placed in the chapel roof) are identical to those of the chapel, and the Hall's present decoration is a deliberate imitation of Wyatt's original plan.

Fig.6: Wyatt's design for the ceiling of the chapel, including the dome: note the contrast with Burges' design and execution (Figs 49 and 50).

For many reasons, Wyatt's chapel was not an entire success. Later generations complained about its dark and dismal feel: it was certainly dimly lit, having only three windows on the south side and one east window of the same size, and its Spartan appeal was rather oddly offset by vast and rather ugly box-like pews and a box-pulpit which had to be dragged into the centre when a sermon was preached. Its grand classical design soon became overlaid with grime and dirt, and gas marks apparently soon covered the stone-coloured paint. Not surprisingly, by the middle of the nineteenth century plans were being discussed about building an entirely new chapel on the west, open, side of the quadrangle. Byzantine architecture was undergoing some renaissance in Western Europe in the 1840s, and this was one of the most popular design plans: the area which is now the Provost's Rose Garden (Fig.7)

Fig.7: The Rose Garden, from above and below, which was where the new (Byzantine) Chapel was intended to go.

---

[14] Ironically, in the light of the 'Victorian High Gothic' nineteenth-century refurbishment, Wyatt himself later experimented with Gothic designs, for example in the chapels at New and Magdalen Colleges, but this was some time after the refurbishment of Worcester Chapel.

would have included a domed and vaulted chapel roof with internal decorations of bright mosaics. In the end, finances prevented the fulfilment of such a vision, in part because at the same time there were similarly elaborate plans to change the cloisters and college frontage. By 1863 George Gilbert Scott (perhaps best known in Oxford for his designs for the Martyrs' Memorial) produced alternative drawings for a restored chapel on the present site: his approach was also Byzantine in style, seeing this as 'the connecting link between Classic and Gothic'.[15] The cost would have been some £6,000: the Fellows turned it down.

The Nineteenth-Century Refurbishment

Yet, only one year later, in 1864, the 'art-architect' William Burges had submitted designs (with a supposed ceiling of £1,500) which were acceptable. Burges was formally a student of civil engineering, like his father, but was increasingly gaining a reputation for refurbishing religious and educational establishments in the style of medieval art and architecture.[16] There were several reasons for the preferment of Burges over Scott. The most obvious – other than that it seemed (at the time) that he would cost the college far less – was that he had several influential friends in Oxford and especially within the Fellowship. One was J.H. Parker, with whom Burges records he occasionally stayed whilst in Oxford, who as a well-known publisher with a particular interest in historic architecture (Parker later became the first keeper of the Ashmolean Museum in 1870) wrote critically about Wyatt's chapel in his 1847 *Handbook for Visitors to Oxford*: his support for Burges' designs undoubtedly influenced the Fellows' decision. Burges' most influential supporters at the time (seen in part by their inclusion in the chapel's iconography) were the two Daniel brothers: Wilson Eustace, who obtained his BA in 1864 and became Scholar and the first Chaplain (actually only for one year) of the refurbished chapel in 1865, and Charles Henry Olive, who was made a Fellow in 1863, later to be Bursar, Dean and, finally, Provost (1903–19). They were both at King's College, London, with Burges. The Revd J.D. Collis, Headmaster of Bromsgrove School and Vicar of Stratford-upon-Avon, was another King's College alumnus and a non-resident Fellow: he, like Henry Daniel, not only supported Burges but additionally gave out of his private means to ensure the completion of the project.

But perhaps a key factor in the acceptance of Burges' designs was his success, over the previous decade, in gaining competitive assignments, both nationally and internationally. The most prestigious was to win a competition of some sixty-three entries for the design of Cork Cathedral (1862). Although work on the cathedral – in which Burges was completely involved – did not properly start until after the reopening of Worcester Chapel in 1864, it was the success of his bold designs, based on French cathedral architecture from the early thirteenth century, and widely recognised as a courageous experiment in French Gothic, which marked a turning point in his career.[17] This achievement,

---

[15] See D. Mordaunt Crook (1981), p. 146.

[16] Those who have informed this section, who have written more widely on Burges' life and influences, include D. Mordaunt Crook (1981) and Charles Handley-Read (1963).

[17] The competition set a ceiling of £15,000 on this project. Burges received strong criticism because he failed to include in his estimate the cost of the towers, spires and carvings; the final cost was closer to £100,000. Had the Fellows of Worcester known this at the time of accepting Burges – who in the end cost them £1,000 more than Scott had estimated – their decision might have been a little different.

compounded with earlier publicity from his winning designs for Lille Cathedral (1855), the Crimea Memorial Church on the Bosphorus (1856), Brisbane Cathedral (1859), Florence Cathedral (1862) and the Bradford Exchange (1863–64) – projects which in each case were never in fact fully executed, but the Fellows of Worcester in 1864 would not know this – undoubtedly gave him increasing prestige. Burges' best known works – Cardiff Castle, Castell Coch, the Harrow Speech Room, Studley Royal, Knightshayes Mansion, the McConnochie's House, Tower House, even Cork Cathedral itself, consecrated in 1870 – were all yet to come; it could be argued that much of what we see in Worcester Chapel was readapted and executed in greater detail in his later assignments. One has only to view the frescoed ceilings of Lady Bute's Bedroom and the carvings in the Drawing Room at Castell Coch (Figs 8 and 9) and the wall friezes in the Summer Smoking Room at Cardiff Castle (where in each case Burges used Thomas Nicholls, the same sculptor who worked on Worcester Chapel) to see the development of Burges' ideas previously expressed on a smaller scale at Worcester (Fig 10).

In fact, the only really tried and tested refurbishment works in process whilst Burges was working on Worcester Chapel (setting aside his unexecuted successes in various competitions) were Salisbury Chapter House, Gayhurst Mansion and Waltham Abbey. In many ways, therefore, the Fellows at Worcester were taking on something of a risk – something which even Henry Daniel realised as the plans were executed and he had to defend what seemed an extravagant and eccentric scheme to critics.

Fig. 8: The mirrored dome with its Oriental flavour in Lady Bute's Bedroom, Castell Coch.

Fig. 9: The Three Fates (amidst flora and fauna) in the Drawing Room, Castell Coch.

So perhaps it was the element of the partially known which actually influenced the acceptance of the chapel designs. Unlike Gilbert Scott, Burges does not appear to have been approached by any other college, and this gave Worcester and its chapel project a certain distinctiveness. Furthermore, although the Fellows (and also the then Provost, Richard Lynch Cotton) were united in their distaste for Wyatt's somewhat depressing chapel, they were certainly not united in what they wanted instead.[18] There was no College consensus in matters Tractarian, despite the general interest in High Gothic Victorian

[19] Some would argue that Burges did indeed owe a debt to Butterfield in his work on All Saints Church, Fleet, Aldershot (1860–62) on account of its polychromy in the brickwork and the Gothic emphases: see C. Handley-Read (1963), p. 194.

[20] It seems that Cotton was a great supporter of Burges' plans for the Chapel, because he saw the importance of transforming Wyatt's cold Classical structure into something more warm and welcoming. His positive view of Burges' plans is recorded in J.W. Burgon (Vol. 2, 1888), p. 86.

Fig.10: The Summer Smoking Room, Cardiff Castle.

architecture amongst some of the Fellows (although he was by no means drawn to Tractarianism, Provost Cotton was married to Edward Pusey's sister, and Henry Daniel served frequently in two High Church ritualistic parishes, St Paul's in Walton Street and St Thomas the Martyr). Hence figures such as William Butterfield (architect of Keble Chapel, 1873–76), with his preference for Gothic spaces and polychromatic decorations, and Arthur Blomfield (architect of the High Victorian Church of St Barnabas, Jericho, 1868–72) would not have satisfied most of the Fellows' tastes.[19] Burges clearly enjoyed the colour and drama of High Church liturgy, more for their representation of the mysterious than for any theological reasons. So although he would not have alienated those with High Church sensitivities (illustrated best in his friendship with Henry Daniel) his wider vision would have also appealed to others as well.

For those who would have preferred a chapel with more Byzantine and exotic Oriental tastes, perhaps regretting that Scott's designs had not been taken up instead, Burges was again a compromise choice. The Fellows would have known of his writings and sketches from Burges' travels to Constantinople and to further parts of the Ottoman Empire and the Far East, especially his designs for the Crimean church on the Bosphorus, which revealed an empathy for Byzantine art and architecture.[20] And for those who preferred – as the College records testify – more 'Italienate [sic] models … after the designs of Raphael in the Vatican'.[21] Burges could qualify here, too: not only his designs for a Florentine Church, but also his many reports and drawings from his stays in Rome, Venice, and Monreale and Palermo, for example, show how these places inspired him in creating his own characteristic fusion between the Middle Ages and Renaissance art and architecture.[22] Furthermore, for those who preferred some continuity with Wyatt's chapel with its more simple and austere Neoclassical Graeco-Roman design, or at the very least a synthesis of Gothic and Classical architecture, Burges again could in part provide what was needed: he had spent time sketching and writing in both Herculaneum and Pompeii, and had travelled quite widely

---

[20] The *Oxford University Herald*, 3 December 1864, records 'when it was determined to undertake the thorough ornamentation and refitting of the Chapel at Worcester College, the Committee placed themselves in the hands of Mr. W. Burges, well-known in connexion with the memorial Church at Constantinople, and one who made colour his special study' (quoted in 'The Chapel' in *The College Record* [1949–50], p. 12).

[21] See the reference in *The College Record* (1949–50), p. 13.

[22] See Mordaunt Crook (1981), p. 147.

in Greece, supported by wealthy patrons such as Lord Bute.[23] His inspiration from classical Rome and Greece could be seen in his designs for the frescos within the antechapel, not only in the geometric patterns, but in the shades and tones of reds, blues and yellows. It would have also been evident in the marble mosaics on the chapel floor (admittedly completed after 1864, but also part of Burges' original designs), where he used techniques he had in part learnt from his earlier apprenticeship with Digby Wyatt and in part had studied when at Pompeii (Figs 11 and 12).[24]

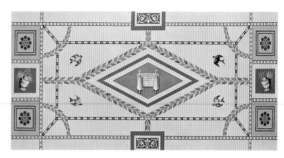

Figs 11 and 12: Two examples of Graeco-Roman influence in the antechapel and on the chancel floor.

Furthermore, Fellows who wanted a newly restored chapel to suggest more contemporary Pre-Raphaelite influence would not have been completely disappointed. Several Pre-Raphaelites, including Rossetti, were among Burges' acquaintances, and many of his sketches for those earlier competitive projects show unmistakable marks of the Pre-Raphaelite school. His eventual commissioning of Henry Holiday, a recognized expert in stained glass who had recently taken over from Edward Burne-Jones at the long-established stained-glass manufacturers James Powell and Sons, and who also worked closely with Morris and Rossetti, shows Burges' concern to include Pre-Raphaelite influence, a feature which is clearly seen in the some of the friezes above the dado and in all the windows of the chapel (Figs 13 and 14).[25]

Burges was also a freemason. At the beginning of his commission he had not yet been initiated as a 'Free and Accepted Mason' in the fashionable Westminster and Keystone Lodge; this took place in 1866, and from that point he passed rapidly through the first three degrees and achieved 'Master Mason' by the end of that year. Burges' earlier associations with freemasonry is evident through his patrons (Lord Ripon was Deputy Grand Master in the 1860s): some would argue that his winning the design for Cork Cathedral was on account of the support of the freemasons of Cork. His use of well-known freemasons such as Thomas Nicholls as sculptor and Henry Holiday for the stained-glass windows for Worcester Chapel reinforces the point.[26]

---

[23] Details of Burges' travels are found in various works by R.P. Pulan (1881–87) quoted in C. Handley-Read (1963), p. 189, who refers to Burges' travels around Europe – and his sketches and notes – from the late 1840s.

[24] See O. Jones (1856, 1986), Chapter V, 'Pompeian Ornament' which (without reference to Burges) illustrates how such designs could have been influenced by Pompeian art. On the chapel floor, see Mordaunt Crook (1981), p. 148.

[25] Burges did not part company with Holiday until 1867, partly for ideological reasons (Holiday could no longer appreciate Burges' attachment to Medieval Gothic expression), but this was long after the completion of the windows in the chapel. Holiday's *Reminiscences* (1914) make much of this rift, describing the way Burges was intrusive and heavy-handed during the refurbishment of the chapel.

[26] A fascinating account of Holiday's role in St Edmund's Masonic Church, Rochdale, is found in the church's website: www.philipcoppens.com/stedmunds.html

Figs 13 and 14: The Pre-Raphaelite angels on Holiday's frieze and window.

For Burges, the structure of Wyatt's chapel echoed not only a Classical Temple – with its cupola, pillars and liturgical spaces – but also the Solomonic temple, with an outer court, an inner court and the Holy of Holies. Wyatt's design was of a 'Temple masking a Church': and the scope for creativity through different allusions to temple architecture, this time using the Solomonic Temple as a prototype, was certainly something which would have attracted Burges, giving him the opportunity to interpret this with a symbolic masonic commentary (Fig.15).

Fig.15: Burges used the image of Solomon several times: here, on the domed ceiling.

And such commentary, sometimes explicit, at others implicit, undoubtedly pervades the Chapel. It is found, for example, in the geometric designs and occasional pentagonal shapes on the frescos (particularly on the south side, near the Provost's Stall, with the illustrations of stones and metals). It is expressed in the black-and-white chequered stones in the mosaic pavement. It is depicted in the interest in the symbolism of 'gates' both leading into and leading out of the chapel, best seen in the figure of Ezekiel above the inner entrance. Here there is a quotation on the scroll from Ezekiel 46 ('*and the people shall worship at the door…*') which is part of a passage describing the prototype new Temple. It is also found in the two illustrations of the Garden of Eden on the ceiling, suggesting masonic ideas that the loss of Eden echoes the loss of the Temple (and hence the need to supplement those losses with a new Temple [Fig.16]). Also on the ceiling, the three personified female virtues of Charity, Hope and Faith, alongside Humility, reflect similar motifs in masonic lodges.[27]

---

[27] For example, the Freemasons' Hall in Lincoln's Inn Fields, London, where the virtues personified in female form are Charity, Hope, Faith, and Truth. See J.S. Curl (1991), p. 112.

Fig.16: 'The Loss of Eden'.

A more esoteric example is in the broken-up, apparently nonsensical, words of the Te Deum, written along the backs of the pews around the entire chapel, which have cryptic word-dividers (':' and 'II') which sometimes spell out in alphabetic code acronyms and abbreviations used by freemasons (such as the Year of Light, the Burning Bush) with hidden references to the various grades of masonic crafts. Other more obvious examples are to be seen in the wood carvings on the pew-ends, which offer several visual representations of masonic crafts – the adze and the nails, the compass, the cross and the rose, the ladder with its nine rungs, and the four-armed cross (Figs 17, 18 and 19).

More implicitly, the colours within the stained-glass windows – the greens, blues, reds, purples, black, white, and crimsons – are not only redolent with theological symbolism, but are also depictions of seven colours of the Seven Masonic Grades. Similarly, the number seven, repeated several times throughout the chapel, echoing the symbolism of creation, when according to Genesis God created the world in seven days, also signifies a most sacred number of freemasonry. Ironically, perhaps the most striking masonic symbol of all is now hidden by the organ, and was exposed only briefly during the chapel's recent restoration: this depicts the pillars of Jachin and Boaz, described in 1 Kings 7:21 as a figurative part of the entrance to Solomon's Temple – Jachin means 'established' and Boaz, 'strength' – and the fresco of these pillars has been placed high up on the western wall in the antechapel (Figs 20 and 21). On the one hand, this contributes to the wealth of Jewish symbolism found there – the bronze laver, also hidden by the organ, is another example of this – but on the other hand, the pillars of Jachin and Boaz are profound and familiar motifs in masonic lodge architecture, where Jachin symbolises the fellowship of the craft, and Boaz, the first degree of apprenticeship, as well as having other more mystical connotations.[28]

[28] See J.S. Curl (1991), pp. 28–32.

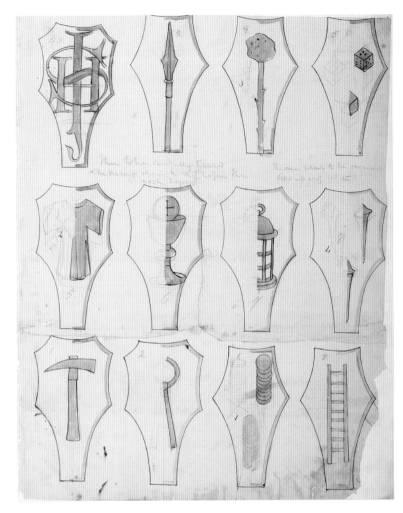

*Figs 17, 18 and 19: The symbolism
in the pew-ends: design and execution.*

Figs 20 and 21: The typically masonic pillars of Jachin and Boaz and the bronze laver, both now hidden behind the organ. The image on the right is of the designs for the bronze laver preserved in the Library.

Other examples suggesting masonic influence include various pagan fertility symbols, particularly popular in the Middle Ages, of the 'green men'; these are partly hidden behind abundant foliage underneath the window recesses, in six of the seven windows (the Crucifixion Window depicts only barren wood), whilst others are inlaid in the ends of some of the stalls, including two on the front of the Preacher's Stall and two on the front of the Chaplain's Stall (Figs 22 and 23).

The general theme of the Chapel, which Henry Daniel some twenty years later had to defend to the Oxford Architectural and Historical Society as 'Man and Nature combine in the Worship of God', could just as well be summed up in the masonic creed as 'Faith in the Grand Architect of the Universe'. The preparatory sketches for the chapel – preserved in the library archives – give further evidence of these interests; the Zodiac designs evident in the designs for the floor of the chapel were actually omitted in the final stages, but the designs of the Ark of the Covenant, and the cherubim, resonant with masonic symbolism, are very much apparent in the antechapel (Fig. 24).[29]

The masonic symbolism can be interpreted theologically, without reference to its significance for freemasonry, and this is clearly what happened, for even Fellows with evangelical leanings were

Fig.22 and 23: The 'Green Men' hidden under the lintels of the windows.

persuaded by Burges' designs. For example, the prophecy-and-fulfilment schema of the chapel windows, and other Jewish and Christian illustrations, would have interested those who had been interested in the millenarianist debates of the 1850s – this was the time of the founding of the MacBride Sermon at Hertford Chapel, for example – and the celebrations of the centenary of the Church Missionary Society, with its emphasis on preaching the Gospel to the Jews as well as to the 'heathen'. Provost Cotton, along with the Principal of Hertford and the Warden of Wadham, was present at the celebrations.[30] Evangelical Scholars and Fellows would have appreciated the key motif of the old order giving way to the new. The scrolls above the windows – a major theme in the following sermons – in part give witness to this 'Jewish Promise/Christian Fulfilment' motif: the scrolls describe an Old Testament prophecy, whilst the windows below reflect an explicit commentary on the fulfilment of this in the life and work of Christ. The entire East Window and accompanying wall panels are also given over to this theme: on the right-hand panel we see a representation of the medieval motif of the blind synagogue, with the ox representing Old Testament sacrifice above it, and a cameo of a bullock being sacrificed beneath it, with the dying lights of a Menorah framing a cameo of the worship of the Golden Calf at the very bottom. On the left-hand side, above the corresponding medieval motif of the seeing church, is the lamb representing the sacrifice of the 'Lamb of God'; below it, on the same level as the animal sacrifice, is the pelican representing the death and resurrection of Christ, with fiery lights of a shining seven-branched candlestick below it, framing this time a cameo of the descent of the Holy Spirit on the disciples in the upper room at Pentecost which is beneath it. With the Crucifixion Window set between these two panels, also with its symbolism of Christian

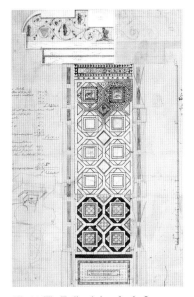

Fig.24: The Zodiac designs for the floor.

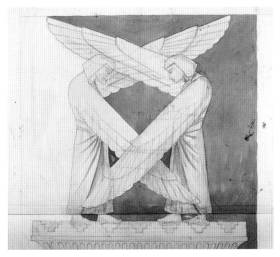

Figs 25 and 26: The design and execution of the cherubim over the Ark.

29 These are found in Burges' 'Report and Book of Designs' held in the College Library; Folder 2: 20–39 no. 24 shows the Zodiac symbols and Folder 2: 20–39 no. 34, the Ark of the Covenant.

30 See J.S. Reynolds (1953), pp. 123–12; S.E. Gillingham (1996), pp. 114–24.

fulfilment of Jewish hope, the contrast between the 'Old Covenant' and the 'New Covenant' could not be more clear (Figs 27 and 28).[31]

More conspicuously, the Jewish symbols painted on the walls in the antechapel – the seven-branched candlestick, the scrolls of law, the incense burners, the high priest Aaron's budding rod, the Ark of the Covenant and the hidden Solomonic pillars and bronze laver – together with the designs of animal skins and curtains, give the impression of entering the Tent of Meeting, through which one passes to enter the Christian Church (Figs 25 and 26). All these give the worshipper a sense of moving through the Old Testament and into the New, the latter illustrated most vividly by the statues of the four Evangelists in the four niches, and the typology of Adam and Eve represented twice, on the ceiling with Christ, and with Mary, Jesus' mother, in the stained-glass windows.[32]

Other Fellows might have appreciated that the dry wit which outlined the theme of 'God and Nature' addressed some of the debates aroused by Charles Darwin's *On the Origin of the Species*, published in 1859. This work challenged the ways in which Genesis had been read more literally, and raised issues about the extent to which the Christian God could also be Creator of the Universe. The famous debate in the Oxford University Museum between Huxley and Wilberforce (Darwin was too ill to attend) had taken place as recently as 1860. Some light-hearted comment on scientific scepticism may well have been intended in Burges' designs – for example in the paintings of non-flying birds, the dodo and kiwi, in the fresco calling upon the 'birds of the air to praise the Lord'; the dodo is again found in the carving on the pew-ends, and as an extinct species adds another touch of humour. The drawings on the fresco which calls upon the 'fishes of the sea' to 'praise the Lord' are of fishes found primarily around the Galapagos Islands; again a touch of humour might have been intended here, as a Worcester alumnus was one of those who accompanied Darwin on HMS *Beagle* in 1831. The pink flamingo – eating fish – would have been another typical comment. Clearly Burges had some pedagogical concerns in the way he covered the chapel with visual imagery, because this evoked the

Figs 27 and 28: 'Seeing Church' and 'Blind Synagogue', to the left and right of the East Window.

Fig.29: Carved wooden monkeys feed off the Tree of Knowledge in Cardiff Castle. Monkeys were a popular Burges motif but were excluded from Worcester Chapel, thus avoiding any commentary on the Oxford controversies about the descent of humankind.

---

[31] The pelican is picked up again in a wood carving on the Chaplain's Stall, with its young feeding on its blood; and the bullock is found again on the Vice-Provost's Stall.

[32] See C. Handley-Read (1961), p. 190. This theme will be brought out later in the sermons.

Figs 30 and 31: The fish of the sea and the beasts of the field 'bless the Lord'.

spirit of the medieval Church and its teaching through pictures, and Burges would have enjoyed a visual reposte in this way (Figs 30 and 31).

Furthermore, some of his smaller designs, for example of tiny birds flying near the ceiling of the chapel and of the minute detail given to some of the flora and fauna on the walls affirm of the design and order in the natural world which suggest the design and order of a Creator (Figs 32, 33 and 34). (The recent restoration of the chapel showed most clearly this impressive attention to detail.) When Samuel Wilberforce, as then Bishop of Oxford, agreed to give the first sermon on the re-opening of the chapel in 1865, his text, which was on the importance of hearing the Voice of God as did the boy Samuel at Shiloh, alluded to these issues more than once. 'For this purpose these walls exhibit to you outlines of all God's creation praising and magnifying their Lord … You know that there is something more than the powers you share with the beasts of the field … that there is something more than this mere material world; yea, that there is more than even mere intellectual capacity, and a voice speaking to that intellect.'[33]

So although it is hard to classify Burges where religion is concerned, because he is more to be defined by what he is not − neither Catholic nor Evangelical, neither broad church nor liberal − his inclusivism and his eclecticism was probably why the Fellows in the 1860s accepted him as a most appropriate choice.

Figs 32, 33 and 34: The Natural Order in praise of God (taken during the 2002 restoration).

[33] See S. Wilberforce (1865), pp. 7 and 8–9.

Fig.35: The four texts over the West Door.

'Burges had turned Wyatt's Neoclassical box into a treasure-chest of ecclesiastical art.' So wrote Mordaunt Crook in 1981.[34] 'He did not obliterate Wyatt's work entirely, but he swamped it.' So Nikolaus Pevsner, a few years earlier.[35] Collis, writing much earlier, was more upbeat: Burges had found a 'room' but left the College 'a chapel ... full of thought, of genius well applied, of symbolism ...'.[36] What is unusual about Burges' contribution to Worcester Chapel, compared with many of his other works before and after this date, was that here he was constrained by the interior alone. His designs for Lille, Florence, Constantinople, Cork – attractive not only because of their topography, but also because of their great towers and spires and domes, which created an immediate visual impact and a sense of suspense as to what might lie within their walls – worked from the impact of the external view to the promise of an internal dimension, where finally the visitor could view that attention to detail which Burges loved. (One has only to think of the Welsh castles, especially the fantasy castle, Castell Coch, to understand quite what a characteristic feature of Burges' designs this was.) By contrast, in Worcester Chapel everything was contained from within, so Burges had to work, with a characteristic attention to the minutest detail, from the inside looking out. There are four texts for one to muse on as one walks out of the chapel: the first, just above the door, as one leaves, is *'Enter His Gates with Thanksgiving'* (Psalm 100). (Is this a comment on the chapel or the world outside?) The second is from a morning psalm (95): *'Today, if you will Hear his Voice, Harden not your Hearts'*. (But is the hearing from within the chapel or outside it?) Just above this is *'O all ye Works of the Lord, bless ye the Lord'*. This is the only call to praise from the Benedicite which has no illustrative frieze underneath it. Who then are the 'works of the

---

[34] J. Mordaunt Crook (1981) p. 152.

[35] See N. Pevsner and J. Sherwood (1974).

[36] In Collis's letter to the high church newspaper, *The Guardian*, (10 June 1872).

Lord'? Are they the congregation about to leave? And the final text, highest of all, is in the scroll held by the prophet Ezekiel: *'And the People shall Worship at the Door'* (Ezekiel 46:3). But why worship on leaving rather than entering? Each of these illustrates Burges' humour and lightness of touch concerning liturgical space (Fig.35).

So what attracted Burges to this project? Was it the medieval origins of this liturgical space, giving him scope to apply his own medieval designs in continuity with its history? Or was it that he enjoyed the challenge of working with Wyatt's structure – because it allowed him to create a particularly Victorian interpretation of what had previously been designed as an early (Roman/Christian) basilica? Certainly the false columns at the west end, the pilasters around the walls, the lunettes over the windows, the dome, the niches in the corners, and indeed the shape of the chapel overall appealed to him, for each had the potential for creating, despite the lack of space, something quite distinctive – that 'Temple within the Church' – which was Classical and Gothic as well.

Whatever the reason, working from the inside outwards, Burges had a great deal of licence. He was able totally to transform and reinterpret the antechapel (probably created by Wyatt to disguise the fact that the entrance to the chapel lay off-centre of the chapel's axis), covering it with Old Testament symbols, giving it space to house the new organ, and yet allowing in this space a sense of anticipation for what lay beyond. Moving into the chapel itself, he was able to take the austerity of Wyatt's walls and cover them from the dado downwards with walnut panelling, and upwards with a frieze and then frescos where he was free to create an elaborate and vivid visual commentary. On a slightly larger scale, he was able to recreate the stucco domed ceiling, working here in some continuity with Wyatt's designs, yet totally transforming them. Burges divided the dome into two compartments, and by adding geometrical mouldings, he was able to use each part for contrasting details. The eastern part he designed in an explicitly theological way – presenting here the Fall of humankind amidst the three Pauline virtues of Faith, Hope and Love (adding a non-Pauline virtue of Humility); the western part he depicted as the consequence of the Fall of humankind – the expulsion from the intimate presence of God in the Garden of Eden – which he set amidst four non-scriptural virtues of Justice, Perseverance, Purity and Moderation. At the angles of the dome Burges returned to the Old Testament/New Testament theme, in the presentations of four important kings of Judah – David, Solomon, Hezekiah and Josiah – each, within the context of the rest of the chapel, to be eclipsed by their successor to the Davidic throne, Christ himself.[37]

Burges was at liberty to fill the empty niches with statues of the Evangelists (a move which created some opposition, as we shall see later). These were inlaid with gilt. In the grisaille above each of them he added a small painting representing an event in each of the Evangelists' lives. For Matthew, Burges depicted the money-changers' table; for Mark, he illustrated the missionary journeys by sea (Figs 36 and 37); for Luke, whose early birth stories focus on the mother of Jesus, he represented the Evangelist painting the Virgin; and for John, he presented the evangelist looking into the empty tomb. In the arabesques at the sides of the niches, he was able to develop these motifs in a different way: Matthew was given the table where money was changed; Mark, a bottle of ink and quill; Luke, a palette and brushes; and John, a chalice and serpent. (Such a

---

[37] The sermons which follow will deal with this in more detail.

Figs 36 and 37: Statues of Mark and Matthew.

human representation of the Evangelists makes it easy to see how and why a few Fellows later saw this in such an anti-iconoclastic way.)

Most importantly, Burges was able to create a visual 'morning chapel', using words and iconic representations of two of the morning canticles (the Te Deum and the Benedicite) – an inspired move, given that daily chapel was mandatory for Fellows and undergraduates at this time, and most would have gone to Matins. Burges was also able to transform the dismal and dark aspect of Wyatt's liturgical space by incorporating on the north side another three windows – an initiative which also allowed him to be creative in the theological use of the number seven (seven windows, seven lunettes,[38] seven frescos and arabesques, seven friezes, seven parts of the Benedicite and the Te Deum, and so on). The additional daylight in his 'morning chapel' also illuminated the windows and frescoes for a congregation which was mostly present in the daylight hours throughout the entire year.[39] Burges developed this schema both vertically and horizontally. From a vertical axis, each of the seven windows had a frieze under it, a decorated wall panel to each side of it, and a lunette with Old Testament prophet and scroll above it; from the horizontal perspective, the words of the Benedicite and the Te Deum were written around the chapel, with the Benedicite picked up again

---

[38] Actually, there are eight lunettes, including Ezekiel's above the West Door, but this does not illustrate a window underneath it.

[39] A practical problem in delivering these sermons at Evensong (which is now the corporate Sunday service, sung by the choir and with a sermon) was that, for at least half of the year, the windows were dark from the outside in and so any comments on their visual impact could not be properly appreciated.

in the wooden animal carvings at the ends of the pews, and the Te Deum taken up in the seven gilt friezes of figures above the dado (and, more implicitly, on the mosaics of the floor) as well as in the group of singers praising God on the alabaster lectern. And, for good measure, Psalm 95, which we have already noted was in part inscribed above the West Door *('Today if you will Hear his Voice, Harden not your Hearts …')* was a morning psalm, assigned for Matins liturgy.

Burges was also able to make a good deal, in his designs at least, of the floor of the chapel, not only in terms of the medium but also its message. If the ceiling represented the degradation of humankind through the depiction of Adam and Eve and their expulsion from Paradise, the floor represented (paradoxically, in terms of space, but rather characteristically fitting Burges' sense of humour) the restoration of the dignity of humanity begun within the church. So on the floor of the chancel Burges inlaid the scene of the sower sowing his seeds (which actually appear to grow outwards not as sheaves of corn, but vine leaves) and on the floor of the chancel the tendrils are woven round six figures representing the apostles, saints, martyrs, evangelists, virgins and confessors. The vine tendrils stop just before the nave; they take root, first, in the four Fathers of the Western Church, and then, further down the chancel, in the twelve kings, scholars, martyrs and builders of the Church in England (Figs 38 and 39).

Burges was also able to create another vertical dimension, in continuity with the floor, in the east end. The tendrils of the plantings (whether corn or vine is unclear) are linked here with the two founders of the Chapel in particular rather than the Church in general. On the north side of the altar is St Benedict, offering (in a typical style of the medieval Church, found, for example, in the royal chapel of Monreale, Sicily, which Burges would have seen) a model of old Gloucester College, giving it back, as it were, to God. On the south side, is Sir Thomas Cookes, similarly presenting a model, this time of Worcester College – again, presenting it to God. In between the two is Holiday's painting of the Entombment. Above this is the Crucifixion Window. Above the window is the lunette, with a text by the prophet Daniel, prophesying the Resurrection. The founders of the two institutions – Benedict representing the specifically religious, Cookes, the more educational – are thus, as it were, transfixed at the foot of the cross (echoing Mary, mother of Jesus and John, in the Crucifixion Window itself), and yet also part, as one looks upwards, of the three main symbols of Christ's Passion.

Figs 38 and 39: The sower and his 'seeds' – the saints of the Western Church.

Fig.40: St Benedict and Sir Thomas Cookes, to the left and the right of the Entombment Frieze.

Burges also attended to the replacement of the cumbersome and ugly box pews. The themes of 'Redemption' and 'Creation' were again developed in these simple and low walnut-wood seats. The theme of the Passion is picked up in the inlays on the ends of the stalls, with symbols such as of the seamless robe, the nails, the crown of thorns, Judas' thirty pieces of silver, and, most unusually, other motifs such as Veronica's Veil, the Seven Wounds of Christ, and, on the Provost's Stall, the Chalice and the Host.[40] More visible, more tangible, more exuberant are the many carved animals on the finials of the pews, signifying the theme of God and Creation: each, with a certain amount of humour, and probably from Burges' view representing a nineteenth-century version of a medieval bestiary, illustrates the animal kingdom in praise of God (Figs 41 and 42).[41]

Figs 41 and 42: The owl (by the Preacher's Stall) and the snake.

[40] Peter Doll (2003), p. 34 makes the point that the latter three especially are 'High Church statements'. But masonic symbols are also found in some of the pew-ends; what is clear is that Burges was not appealing to one part of the church alone in any of his decoration.

[41] An apt quotation ascribed to Burges is as follows: 'There are some people who … consider mediaeval art as eminently ecclesiastical, and therefore profoundly serious to be approached with caution, forgetting that mankind has been very much the same in every age, and that our ancestors joked and laughed as much as we do.' See www.achome.co.uk/williamburges

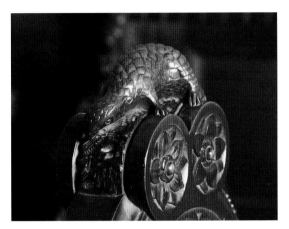

Fig.43: The Provost's Stall with the lion and the lamb as armrests, and the pangolin; the inscription 'God' is the backrest.

Fig.44: The Vice-Provost's Stall with the tortoise; the inscription 'Raise' is the backrest.

Another example of Burges' humour is found especially in the Provost's and Vice-Provost's stalls. In the former, the words of the Te Deum are so spaced out so that the word 'God' is placed in the heart of the Provost's Stall. An animal carving of the spiny long-nosed pangolin is on one of the pew-ends, hinting at the need for the gift of being 'thick-skinned', with its long nose designed for sniffing out trouble; the carvings of the lion and the lamb on the hand-rests have connotations of the hope for a just and peaceful regime. As for the Vice-Provost, the word 'raise' (broken up from the word 'praise') is found in an identical position to 'God', suggesting in this case some hope for preferment. The animal carving of the slow-but-sure tortoise as one of the two pew-ends confirms this interpretation. Add to this the carving of the unicorn (with its questions about the 'truth and myth' of the Gospel) and that of the cockerel (reminding us of the denial of Peter during the trial of Christ) in the Chaplain's Stall, and the wise owl in the stall for visiting preachers, and it is clear that satirical comment was intended.[42]

The following sermons are primarily based on the chapel's windows, but they are very much dependent upon the general impact of the rest of the chapel's iconography for their meaning. Burges designed the (now seven) windows under the theme of 'Christ, the Light of the World'. The sub-themes in the schema were both 'Revealed Religion' (expressed explicitly through the stained glass, but repeated below the windows in the friezes illustrating the Te Deum above the dado, and repeated again in the lunettes above the windows, with their scrolls highlighting the words of various prophets) and also 'Natural Religion' (expressed in the frescos and arabesques on the walls on each side of the windows, illustrating the words of the Benedicite). Burges changed the order

[42] The mid-1860s were rife with theological uncertainties. First, Darwin (1859 and 1860) and the questions about the proper relationship between science and religion; second, the publication of *Essays and Reviews* (1860) by a number of prominent Oxford theologians, which questioned the nature of the historical accounts of Jesus of Nazareth and, behind those, the Old Testament stories; and third, the debates within the church itself about the appropriate interpretation of tradition, whether biblical, church-traditional, or more rational. Given Burges' pedagogical concerns, some interaction with these issues through the iconography was almost certainly intended.

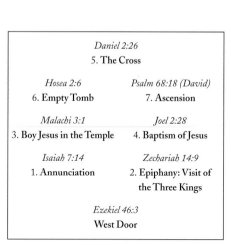

Daniel 2:26 5. The Cross	
Hosea 2:6 6. Empty Tomb	*Psalm 68:18 (David)* 7. Ascension
Malachi 3:1 3. Boy Jesus in the Temple	*Joel 2:28* 4. Baptism of Jesus
Isaiah 7:14 1. Annunciation	*Zechariah 14:9* 2. Epiphany: Visit of the Three Kings
Ezekiel 46:3 West Door	

Fig.45: The final arrangement of the windows.

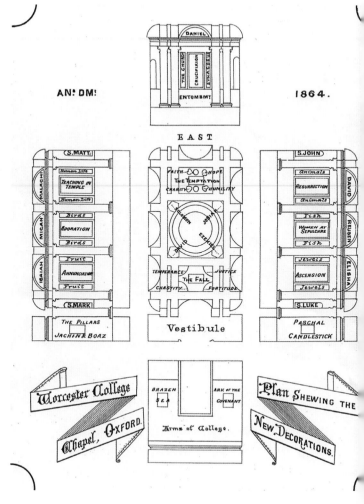

Fig.46: The Chapel design a. presented in The Gentleman Magazine *(1864).*[44]

of these windows several times, as well as his choice of the prophetic figures in the lunettes above each of them.[43] The recent restoration brought into view earlier scriptural verses on some of the scrolls as well as previous renditions of prophetic figures, still apparent under the present ones. The reproduction (Fig.46) shows the earlier order, published in *The Gentleman's Magazine* (1864); the whole design also reveals a much stronger Jewish Hope/Christian Fulfilment appeal, both in the additional features in the antechapel and the design of the chancel. The final arrangement of the windows and prophetic texts can be seen in Fig.45: we may note here a much more subtle chronological and aesthetic appeal, both in the arrangement of the windows on each side of the chapel and the repetition and contrast of some key themes between one window and another.

The chronological theme of the windows is, from the West Door, and working from the north to the south (or left to right) the birth of Jesus (Annunciation and Epiphany); formative beginnings of Jesus' ministry (as a boy in the Temple, at his Baptism); and the resurrection of Jesus (the Empty

---

[43] Burges originally chose as his artist for the windows the Pre-Raphaelite glazier J.E. Millais, but his first commission, of the 'Adoration of the Magi', Burges found unacceptable. Henry Holiday was chosen instead. The windows were completed by the late 1860s, although Holiday's work on the other murals and the frieze illustrating the Te Deum took some time longer – during which time Holiday and Burges had parted company, mainly because Burges refused to give Holiday any artistic freedom. Holiday never worked for him again.

[44] P. Doll (2003), pp. 33–34 argues that the east window was once intended to be a scene of the Last Judgement, more in common with Roman Catholic and Byzantine Churches; it is possible that Burges once painted a watercolour with this schema, with the crucifixion scene where the entombment painting is now. Whether this was seen as reflecting Tractarian influence (seen for example in the dominance of this theme in Keble Chapel and at St Barnabas, Jericho) is difficult to know. But the Crucifixion Window is present in both the earliest published plans and continued as part of the final scheme.

Fig.47: Burges' plans for the Chapel walls.   *Fig.48: Execution of plans for the walls.*

Tomb and Ascension), with the Crucifixion Window, above the altar, dominating the entire scene. The windows also have an interesting aesthetic arrangement. The first and last windows on the north side (the Annunciation and the Empty Tomb) both feature angelic figures mediating their message to a woman – one to Mary of Nazareth at Jesus's birth, the other to Mary of Magdala at Jesus's death – and each is configured in a very similar way. Similarly, the first and last windows on the south side (the Epiphany and the Ascension), which are both arranged around the theme of the human and divine kingship of Jesus Christ, feature distinct compositions of figures gazing on him (the three kings on the Infant Christ, the six disciples on the Risen Christ) as each group struggles to determine who he is and what his Kingship is really about.[45]

Burges' transformation of Wyatt's chapel could be illustrated in many different ways. A good example is to contrast some of his designs with those offered earlier by Wyatt, i.e. of the west door, the walls, and the ceiling (Figs 4, 5 and 6). The differences, highlighted by the recent restoration of the chapel, are striking (Figs 47 and 48; 49 and 50).

It is not surprising that Burges emerged from this project with both friends and foes. Amongst the latter were those who objected to his designs for theological reasons and those who complained on financial grounds. Amongst the former were those who, acknowledged his reputation by the 1870, and sought a corresponding design for the Dining Hall.

---

[45] The ways in which this arrangement impinges upon the theological message of the Chapel as a whole will be brought out in the sermons on each of these particular windows.

Fig.49: Burges' design for the chapel dome.   *Fig.50: Execution of the design for the chapel dome.*

Those who opposed Burges for theological reasons were mainly preoccupied with the statues of the Evangelists in the corners of the chapel, and their propensity to attract idolatrous worship. By 1865 the lawyers of Lincoln's Inn, instigated by the then librarian of Worcester, Edmund Oldfield, joined the fray by publicly denouncing the statues as 'idolatrous'. Oldfield took the view that had these statues been of 'Faith, Hope and Charity and the like …' there would have been no problem because no veneration would have been intended. By 1866, using various scriptural invectives, such as the (perhaps somewhat antiquated) anti-pagan teaching in Deuteronomy 7:6, the Revd Charles Browne, another Fellow, appealed to Provost Cotton that these superstitious images would encourage the young men of the college to assume such abominations which would to lead to 'sensuous and carnal worship'. The Attorney General, Sir Roundell Palmer, was brought in. Rather cleverly he pronounced – answering the invective of Oldfield – that the statues were not so much about 'worship' as about 'decoration'. They were no more, no less, a composite part of the chapel decoration, and so had no idolatrous associations. The whole debacle could not but produce some public satire: one example, now preserved in the SCR, is by H.C. Liddell, inscribed in pen and ink. The date of the chapel's redecoration coincided with Bouverie's Bill for the abolition of tests for university (in other words, the necessity of would-be members having to subscribe to the thirty-nine Articles of the Church of England). Thus the cartoon is of the Fellows (now at last liberated) worshipping many and various strange idols – the Koran and *Essays and Reviews* are two which are clearly marked. At the front is Provost Cotton in flight, wishing, it is assumed, that Burges had never taken on this formative task in encouraging liberation in the first place. The cartoon can be seen on the opposite page (Fig.51).

The opposition to the economic costs of Burges' plans was also quite clear. The ceiling of £1,500 initially came out at twice that amount (although nowhere near as exorbitant as the costs for Cork Cathedral). This was still far less than the quotation for George Scott's designs. However, the 'completion' of the chapel's refurbishment in 1864 was something of a misnomer: the final costs

Fig.51: The Fellows worshipping false gods, inspired by the Chapel's 'idolatrous' iconography.

came out at £7,000 – ironically £1,000 more than those of Scott – and, perhaps predictably, some Fellows thought this was too much for the price, whilst others – recognising the unique flavour Burges had given to the Chapel – actually persuaded him, at a somewhat more modest cost, and with the pressure of Henry Daniel behind it, to offer proposals for a new design for the Hall.

This took place in the 1870s. On this occasion Burges had to face a great deal of compromise in the execution and cost of his original scheme, so that only half of the refurbishment of Wyatt's walls and ceilings and windows was eventually allowed. Although this may well have been a later vote of continued confidence in Burges, the irony is that whilst his controversial refurbishment of the chapel has nevertheless been preserved up to the present day without modification, that of the Hall, by contrast, has resulted in repeated alterations – in 1909, in 1927–28, in the 1950s and, finally, in the 1960s when, with generous financial help from his descendant, Woodrow Wyatt MP, an alumnus of Worcester, a return to Wyatt's designs for the Hall meant that any evidence of Burges there was all but eroded (until, that is, the recent restoration of Burges' East Window above the high table.)

Hence for those who enjoy the audacity and complexity of Burges' work, only the chapel has survived to give testimony to his artistic and architectural skills. Although his influence here has continued for nearly a hundred and fifty years, on three occasions some renovation has been deemed essential in order to preserve Burges' designs and to bring the nineteenth-century colours back to life. The chapel was cleaned in 1949 (when the attempts to remove the dirt and grime of the previous eighty years with 'Chemico' Household Cleaner achieved a dramatic scouring, but to the detriment of the loss of much surface paint and then some residual dust caking). In 1981 the east end wall was cleaned and given a rather thick protective wax coating. The major restoration took place in 2002. For this, Cliveden Conservation Workshop removed with far greater sensitivity and professionalism the dirt and the protective coverings which, through previous efforts, had obliterated the brightness of the designs. They also reinforced the original ceiling ribs and mouldings in the walls, and most especially retouched with immense attention to detail all the gilding and ceiling and wall paintwork and woodwork.[46] The final outlay on the chapel itself was some £230,000, made possible by generous legacies from Dr John Walker and Professor Robert Martin, whose names are recorded in a Latin plaque opposite the organ. (This was

---

[46] The full report, dated 2002, by Cliveden Conservation Workshop, with its many illustrations of the details (Figures 1–61), shows the extent of the restoration and the ways in which the most intricate details were once again restored to their 1860s glory.

considerably less, in comparative terms, than was eventually paid out for Burges' original designs, some £7,000). But for those who remember the chapel as it was in the twentieth century and compare it with what it has become in the twenty-first, the difference speaks for itself. As well as the dramatic overall effect of the colours, the minute attention to Burges' details – of birds, flora, fauna and geometric designs, of the scrolls of the prophets above the windows, of the friezes beneath the windows, of the frescos in the antechapel and on each side of the windows, of the gold and gilt within the domed ceilings – has had stunning results. The chapel was covered in scaffolding for the best part of a year; but the contrast of its appearance before and after has been dramatic (compare Fig.52 with the full-page image on page 42).

Visual Exegesis

One of the greatest challenges for a preacher is how to give ancient texts contemporary relevance. In the attempt to merge the horizons of the world of the text and the world of the congregation, a preacher has to overcome at least two obvious obstacles: the culture of the biblical texts is often so unfamiliar (for example, in its different views about slavery, polygamy, idolatry, warfare, sex and gender), whilst twenty-first century listeners are preoccupied with questions of which the

Fig.52: The Chapel c.1864 (from the Amphlett Diaries, 1906).

biblical writers were totally unaware (scientific experimentation, climate change, financial markets, family breakdown, and so on). There are of course many shared concerns of a more fundamental nature – about the nature and effects of human wickedness and human goodness, and about how and why God is found to be both present and absent in our world – and the art of a good sermon is to search for what is familiar and to explicate what is not. Preaching with too much emphasis on the historical background of the text can result in its becoming increasingly distant, and focusing too much on contemporary issues can make the text seem irrelevant or superfluous.

Visual exegesis is one way of offering a creative bridge between these two horizons. Artistic representations of Scripture are of course later interpretations with little if no verbal explanation (occasionally texts are also added, as is the case with Burges' designs for the chapel), and because they reflect the concerns of yet another 'intermediate' age from that of the text and that of a contemporary audience they serve as a visual bridge between the world of the Bible and the world of the contemporary observer. In effect, the artist has taken something which was essentially diachronic (that is, set 'within time', written in an ancient language and for a specific purpose) and, by releasing

Fig.53: The Chapel 2002 (during restoration).

it from the specificity of language, made it more synchronic (that is, understood and interpreted beyond the confines of the written text).[47]

Visual representations are an excellent way of allowing the intellect to work alongside the imagination. What is appealing about Burges' iconography is that his concern was not only to please but also to instruct, so both elements work together within his designs for the chapel. Burges was interested in both these aspects because he identified so much with the art and architecture of the Middle Ages, when instruction for a more illiterate laity was achieved through the art forms of stained glass, sculpture and painted canvas. This means that a contemporary preacher can use Burges' visual interpretations (taken through a nineteenth-century lens) and through these look back to the biblical source.[48] The result is a constant 'trialogue' between the biblical text, Burges' various artistic interpretations of that text, and the preacher's understanding of both text and artist, a process which can both enrich and enlighten the text, the preacher and the congregation.

As far as Worcester Chapel is concerned, however, Burges was not only interested in instruction through decorative symbolism but also in instruction through words. These are over the West Door, under the Crucifixion Window, in the prophets' scrolls, in the Benedicite and Te Deum, and, in Latin, on the floor of both the chancel and nave. The result of seeing both 'text' and 'picture' is that it is often hard for the preacher to know whether to use the texts with the iconography as illustration, or the iconography with the texts as explanation. Does one start with the visual or with the exegetical? Does one work from the imagination to the intellect, or *vice versa*?

In the sermons I have used a two-pronged approach. When the text illustrating the visual is used minimally (as in the seven windows and their scrolls), I have started with the visual and worked back to the text. When the text is more dominant I have started with the text and worked forward to the visual (as in the case of the two canticles which surround the entire chapel). This means that sometimes one is 'giving words to the pictures' and at other times, 'picturing the words'.

---

[47] Obviously visual representation is not the only way in which this can happen: poetic imitation, musical and dramatic representation and narrating the stories in modern idiom are the most obvious other examples. The emphasis here is on visual exegesis, because this has been the key concern in the sermons.

[48] Burges was interested in church history as well as biblical history for his iconographical allusions to the Christian tradition, so both Bible and Church are the sources as far as the chapel is concerned.

'Visual exegesis' has become an important discipline in academic theology. In the field of reception history, for example, there is an increasing awareness of the important interface between theological commentary and art history.[49] Theological commentary is most effective when it appeals both to the intellect in its exegetical and diachronic concerns and to the imagination in its theological and synchronic concerns.[50] Visual imagery is obviously one important means to this end, bringing together many different elements of the text into one space – as Burges himself does – thus allowing for a more diverse and multi-layered commentary.[51] So the following sermons are in fact a practical application of what already interests me within an academic context: in them I try to combine 'narrative exegesis' (looking *at* biblical texts and themes) and 'visual exegesis' (looking *through* the images via the artists to perceive their effect on us today).

Any visual exegesis of Worcester Chapel has to deal with the bigger picture as well as giving attention to detail. Working on these sermons over several years I have become increasingly aware of the importance of the extraordinary symmetry in the imagery of the chapel as a whole. Take, for example, the repetition of the number *four*: the most obvious is in the four statues in the four corners with the four paintings and the four arabesques above them. In addition there are the two pairs of round pillars at the west and east end, the fourfold schema on the ceiling, which is repeated twice (the four Christian virtues and the four Classical virtues) with the four kings of Israel round the outside of the dome between them; and, similarly, the fourfold schemas on the floor, represented by four saints of the Western Church nearest the altar and three groups of four saints of the English Church from the lectern towards the West Door. A second example of numerical symmetry is Burges' emphasis on the mystical number *seven* – the seven windows, the seven scrolls above them, the seven archetrypes, and the seven friezes around the dado, for example. Whereas the number four is found on the ceiling and floor and in the corners, the number seven is found on the walls. A further example is the recurrence of the number *twelve*. Each of Holiday's six friezes under the windows on the north and south walls has twelve figures; the Benedicite is divided into twelve parts – three at the west end, three at the east end, and three down each side; and on the ceiling, the four Classical virtues, four Christian virtues and four kings of Israel make up twelve cameos, whilst on the floor, the three groups of four saints of the English church echo the same number. Even the sculpture on the lectern numbers twelve singers, all in classical attire. All these numbers have theological significance, each in different ways representing completion and order, and each providing an ordered visual framework for attending to the greater elaboration of detail. It would seem that for Burges, form, symmetry and repetition provided a way of organising and ordering what initially might seem to the viewer to be chaotic exuberance.

Because these sermons, originally heard, have been transposed into a written form, it has still been possible to retain the visual, but impossible (at least, without an accompanying CD) to retain

---

[49] See for example R. Viladesau (2000); W.A. Dryness (2001); J.F.A. Sawyer (ed.) (2006); N. O'Hear (2008).

[50] See N. O'Hear (2008) pp. 338–42, discussing Gadamer and Davey's distinction between 'Vorstellung' (a more literal representation usually communicated through texts) and 'Darstellung' (a visual response which encourages more the involvement of the spectator to add something to what is already there).

[51] The other element of this is of course music; I shall return to this at the end of this section.

the auditory, musical setting which brought them to life. The sermons were superbly enhanced by the chapel choir, with their most appropriate choice of psalms and anthems and their consistently high standard of rendering them – whether by the mixed choir, or the male choir – which provided another type of 'encounter' with the art of the chapel just before the sermon began. Although there are few explicit references to the chapel's music in the sermons themselves, I nevertheless am indebted to the choirs of Worcester College Chapel, to the several Organ Scholars and to the two Directors of the Chapel Music, Andrew Gant and Stephen Farr, who served during the six years the sermons evolved.[52]

I am equally grateful for the support of the two chaplains, the Revd Dr Peter Doll and the Revd Emma Pennington, who invited me to preach these sermons at different occasions in the university year. One was at an (Advent) Carol Service, another was at a service of the Induction of the new Scholars, another was a Remembrance Sunday. Others were part of a Sermon Series – an eight-week series on the Lord's Prayer, a series on the Seven Deadly Sins, a series on the Beatitudes, and another on the titles for Jesus in the Gospel of John. The positive aspect of this was that the sermons served the life of the Chapel in all its diversity; the downside was that sometimes it seemed as if one was trying to do two things at once – deal with a specific liturgical occasion *and* deal with the subject of the windows themselves.

The sermons are not presented here in the order they were given, but rather in the order that makes most sense within the iconography of the chapel; so the first is the Benedicite, then the Annunciation Window, then the Epiphany, and then the Presentation of Christ in the Temple, then the Baptism, then the Crucifixion, then the Empty Tomb, then the Ascension, and finally the Te Deum.

Fig.54: Touching up the scroll of Malachi during restoration.

52 For further insights on the chapel and its music, see www.worcesterchapel.co.uk/index which gives information about the choirs, their recordings, the history of Worcester Chapel, and the people.

The Benedicite

14 October 2002
Reading: Daniel 3: 23–68 (Apocrypha)

The Benedicite was sung by the Choir as the Evening Anthem (Dyson in F).

The last time I preached in this chapel was on the Garden of Eden story, which was a rather difficult feat, as the two images of Adam and Eve on the ceiling which I was using as illustrations were almost completely hidden by scaffolding. But what a transformation it all is: the restoration

Daniel holds his scroll.

has brought to light so much which had previously been hidden by dust and dirt, and now we see everything so distinctly: the tiny details of the birds and fishes, the vibrant colours, the gilt writing, the carved walnut woodwork. It has brought to life a rich tapestry of theological themes and biblical symbols; so much so that I decided to rise to the challenge of offering a series of sermons on the iconography of the Chapel, of which this is in effect the first.

You might well argue that I am looking at the decorations in the chapel only with the biased eyes of a biblical theologian, and that William Burges, the nineteenth-century designer and architect, never intended so many allusions. I wonder. Burges did not always receive approval for his tastes from the Fellows of this College; so his interest in bizarre and exuberant imagery – as well as his clear sense of humour – was in part given a certain orthodox expression through his use of biblical symbols. Take the figure of Daniel, for instance: we know that there were two 'Daniels' in College at the time of Burges' commission (in 1863) and they both supported Burges in his enterprise. They were, after all, brothers, and had been

Benedict with Saint Olaf – or Olive Daniel?

to the same school as Burges and had followed his growing reputation with interest. Wilson Eustace Daniel was a Scholar and the first Chaplain of the refurbished chapel in 1865, and Charles Henry Olive Daniel was a Fellow (and some forty years later became Provost). 'Olive' Daniel's red beard and hair are immortalised on the frieze just beyond the Vice-Provost's Stall – he has become the Norwegian warrior-saint 'Olaf'. William Daniel, priest and College Chaplain, may well be represented by the figure of the Old Testament Daniel in the iconography above the altar. So in these two iconic images we see Burges' humour and his contemporary use of biblical and ecclesiastical themes.

We shall return to Daniel shortly. An important point to note first is that, even if Burges did use Old Testament themes freely, he probably did so because this echoed the many artistic representations of the Old Testament in the Middle Ages. This period appealed to him most. 'I was

The pelican   *The unicorn*

brought up in the thirteenth-century belief, and in that belief I intend to die', he wrote in 1876. Visual symbolism in art and architecture would have edified ordinary medieval congregations more than the sung, read and preached words. Because of the low level of literacy and the medium of Latin liturgy, the laity in the fourteenth century (at about the time when the first Benedictine community arrived on this site) were taught as much by what they *saw* as by what they *heard*. Burges empathises with the medieval appeal to the mind through the eye. Liturgical space was a pleasing challenge of demonstrating how iconography could be both aesthetically pleasing and instructional at the same time.

Burges had a profound sense that God could be found in the created order of things – what some theologians have termed 'Natural Religion'. For Burges, this was part of his masonic belief in 'the Great Architect of the Universe'. This was an important complement to 'Revealed Religion', which in Christian terms emphasises that God is found essentially through the birth, death and resurrection of Christ. This chapel bears ample testimony to religion both 'Natural' and 'Revealed'. The best examples are seen in the choice of the two Morning Canticles whose words encompass the entire chapel. The Benedicite runs round the cornice – most of you will be able to read of some of it quite clearly – which calls upon all the created order to 'bless the Lord'. The Te Deum runs around the Dado at the backs of your pews against the wall, so is more difficult to read; this is a hymn calling upon all the church to give praise to God. So through these two canticles all Nature and all the Church join to give praise to God who is both Creator and Redeemer.

The themes of the Benedicite and the Te Deum are reiterated in other parts of the chapel. Take, for example, the pews where you are sitting. The walnut carvings on the armrests echo the Benedicite, in that the animals of the created order are depicted praising God: look for the humorous touches again in the dodo, the pelican and – by the Chaplain's Stall – the unicorn and cockerel.

The Crown of Thorns

The hammer

Meanwhile, the pew-ends pick up by contrast symbols of Chirst's suffering and so echo the Te Deum – the Cross and Crown of Thorns, for example, are two of these.

The same two themes of the Natural Order and the Revealed Order are also represented on the domed ceiling. Nearest the altar you can see four virtues which are associated with biblical, revealed religion – Faith, Hope, Humility and Charity; nearest the door are illustrations of four virtues which symbolise 'Natural Religion' – Justice, Perseverance, Purity, Moderation.

We shall reflect on the Te Deum and the importance of 'Revealed Religion' another time. For the rest of this sermon I want to focus on the Benedicite, whose theme of 'Natural Religion' pervades all the walls of the chapel. Some would argue that, given the context of the 1860s, when these designs were made, they are in part a humorous and defiant response to the questions about God as Creator in the wake of Charles Darwin's recent publications on natural selection. The development of these debates continues in Oxford today: so Burges' commentary on the entire Natural Order – animals and humans alike – being a witness to God as Creator is not simply a commentary determined only by nineteenth-century concerns, but has an impact on us as well.

Four Christian Virtues (and Adam and Eve tempted in Eden).

Four pagan Virtues (and Adam and Eve fleeing from Eden).

The Benedicite is presented throughout the chapel in twelve parts: twelve calls of praise are written continuously on the cornice, and seven of these are illustrated on the wall panels which frame the stained-glass windows found directly beneath them. The restoration has enabled us to see the gilt details of the actual text: most of you will be able to see at least one example of the repeated refrain 'bless the Lord'. (The words in Latin are 'Benedicite Domino': its use in Christian worship has given it the short title, Benedicite.)

The Benedicite's first call to 'bless the Lord' is under the scroll of Ezekiel, above the west entrance: 'O all ye works of the Lord, bless ye the Lord' ('Benedicite, omnia opera Domini, Domino'). Because this is directly above the entrance, there is no illustrative wall panel: it is as if those within the congregation who pass below become the 'living frieze'. A contrasting call is at the east end of the chapel, above the altar: 'O ye Priests of the Lord, bless ye the Lord.' (Is this deliberately set below Daniel, new Chaplain of Worcester, Priest of the Lord?) Under this is the Crucifixion Window, and on each side are wall panels developing this theme – on the one side, symbols of Jewish priesthood are found, and on the other, images of Christian priesthood are represented.

On each side of this 'altar call' are two other calls to praise similar to this: one focuses on earthly praise, the other on heavenly: 'O ye Servants of the Lord, bless ye the Lord'… 'O ye Angels of the Lord, bless ye the Lord'. There is actually no window under each of these; the wall paintings on each side of the Gospel figures are kept to the minimum.

In the other two corners, at the west end, the call to 'bless the Lord' is extended to the Natural Order. One is a very general appeal: 'O ye Light and Darkness, bless ye the Lord'. The other is the specific corollary of it: 'O ye Nights and Days, bless ye the Lord'. As with the two corners at the east end, the wall panels, again flanking the statues of the Gospel Writers, are quite restrained.

When we come to the side walls to the north and south the iconography is much more developed. On each side are three calls to praise, making six scenes in all. Each call to 'bless the Lord' is set above a stained-glass window, and, like the east window, the wall panels on each side of

On the north wall the calls to bless the Lord are addressed respectively to the 'Green Things', the 'Fowls of the Air' and the 'Children of Men', with the frescos below echoing the same motifs.

On the south wall, the calls to bless the Lord continue, addressed to the 'Beasts and Cattle', the 'Seas and Floods'
and the 'Mountains and Hills', each reflected in the details of the frescos on each side of the window.

the window illustrate these six themes in considerable detail. First, on the north side the Earth itself is summoned to praise: 'O all ye Green Things upon the Earth, bless ye the Lord' The refurbishment has brought out the delicate decoration of the grapes and tropical fruits, perhaps with that touch of humour typical of dessert at an Oxford high table.

The second call addresses the skies to join the praise: 'O all ye Fowls of the Air, bless ye the Lord'. Again, the renovation has shown up the tiny birds in flight close to the ceiling, as well as the flamingo and the heron, lower down, and, typical of Burges' humour, the dodo and the kiwi, neither of which could fly.

The final call on the north side is to all of humanity: 'O ye Children of Men, bless ye the Lord' The panel shows up the small but striking white cameos of clusters of figures, such as a king, a doctor, a soldier, a poet, a lawyer, a carpenter, a mother, a fisherman – all parts of society and not just the church – being called upon to bless their Creator.

On the south side of the chapel, opposite the call to the 'Children of Men' is the call to 'All ye Beasts and Cattle, bless ye the Lord'. Again we see Burges' lightness of touch in the depiction of the wild beasts, such as a tiger, and a kangaroo with its baby, with the smaller animals, such as the porcupine and mouse. (Additional images of the 'Beasts and Cattle' are illustrated in a different form in the carved walnut wood on the pew-ends.)

The next call reads 'O ye Seas and Floods, bless ye the Lord'. Here, Burges has depicted tiny fishes (with the same amount of detail he presented the tiny birds on the opposite wall panel) alongside Leviathan, the great sea monster, all purportedly praising God.

The final summons to praise, nearest the west door, reads 'O ye Mountains and Hills, bless ye the Lord'. Here the illustrations on each side ot the window are more symbolic – of gemstones and minerals, arranged in strange geometric designs, with some hints of alchemy here.

Some would argue that this schema is just an amusing, but rather bland appeal (these days of a fairly liberal New Age kind) to the Created Order to recognise its Creator. But the Benedicite can trace its origins to early Christian liturgy: it was certainly well known when, in the sixth century, the Rule of Benedict (Chapter Twelve) stipulated its use every Sunday in the Office of Lauds. Along with the Te Deum, it would have been a regular part of Sunday worship for the Benedictine community who occupied this site from the late thirteenth century onwards. Far from being overly modern and frivolous, the canticle has a serious orientation. Its origins actually go back into the Old Testament: but not from the creation story in Genesis – although the ideas of God separating light and darkness, earth and seas, and creating vegetation, fish, birds, cattle, and so on all have influenced the author – nor from the Psalms, although the repeated calls there to 'bless the Lord' may also have influenced the work.

As we heard from our first lesson tonight, and heard yet again in our anthem, the Benedicite actually comes from an additional part of the Old Testament called the Apocrypha, and is placed in the book of Daniel. It has been excluded from the inner core of the Old Testament because the earliest manuscript is in Greek, and only the texts in Hebrew were initially acceptable as part of the inner 'canon'. The Benedicite was originally a song ascribed to 'The Three Young Men' – heroes of faith like Daniel himself, whose story of being thrown to the lions is one of the best remembered in the Bible. These three young men were thrown into a fiery furnace by a Babylonian king called

Nebuchadnezzar, where they saw a protecting angel ('one like a son of the gods'), and where – so the heroic folktale goes – they sang this song. So in its original setting this is not a bland hymn 'anthropomorphising' creation, but is an act of defiant faith in the midst of a terrifying crisis, both physical and spiritual.

Burges intended his architectural symbols to be as much for edification as for aesthetic pleasure, so there is undoubtedly an important twenty-first century message in this call on all Creation to bless God. This message – and here of course I cannot be fully sure that this was what Burges intended – is intrinsic to its setting in Daniel (and fits well with the plays on the two Daniel brothers elsewhere in the chapel). In its context, in that Old Testament book, it is a bold song which praises God for his goodness and order in Creation, even when faced with the horrific reality of human wickedness. Given all we have seen of this since '9/11', surely this has something to teach us at this point in world history.

This belief in one Creator, God of all Creation, natural and human, is shared by all monotheistic faiths, whether Jew, Christian, or Muslim. Through the different mediums of our 'Revealed Religion', God has many names. He is 'the Father of our Lord Jesus Christ'; He is Yahweh, Adoni, or 'ha-shem' – 'the name'; He is Allah. But through the shared medium of 'Natural Religion', together we acknowledge him as our Creator God – of light and darkness, of night and day, of green things and beasts and cattle, of seas and floods, of mountains and hills. The Benedicite stresses the equality and interdependence of everything and everyone, great or small, within the Created Order, a theme which Burges depicted so well and so typically, first in the large expanse of his canvas, then in the minute, intricate details.

A radical implication arises from this. 'Revealed Religion', whether Christian, Jewish or Muslim, is necessarily more exclusivist because of its beliefs in a special revelation, and such religious sectarianism often incites those awful calls to 'Holy War', the effects of which we know so well today. But 'Natural Religion', with its belief in the equality of all peoples and the universality of divine love – for Christian, Jew and Muslim alike – has the potential to be an inspiration for world peace. The Benedicite depicts a religion shared naturally by all who acknowledge God as their Creator, in good times and bad.

'O all ye Works of the Lord, bless ye the Lord.' Next time you see these words above you as you leave the Chapel, spare a thought on what they could and should mean for all of us – Christians, Jews, Muslims alike – who are included in that call to praise, a call which can uplift our shared faith in God our Creator – not only when things go well, but also when they go dreadfully wrong. 'O ye Light and Darkness, bless ye the Lord'.

Appendix: The Words of the Benedicite
The Benedicite (from The Book of Common Payer)

O all ye Works of the Lord, bless ye the Lord : praise him, and magnify him for ever.

O ye Angels of the Lord, bless ye the Lord : praise him, and magnify him for ever.

O ye Heavens, bless ye the Lord : praise him, and magnify him for ever.

O ye Waters that be above the Firmament, bless ye the Lord : praise him, and magnify him for ever.

O all ye Powers of the Lord, bless ye the Lord : praise him, and magnify him for ever.

O ye Sun and Moon, bless ye the Lord : praise him, and magnify him for ever.

O ye Stars of Heaven, bless ye the Lord : praise him, and magnify him for ever.

O ye Showers and Dew, bless ye the Lord : praise him, and magnify him for ever.

O ye Winds of God, bless ye the Lord : praise him, and magnify him for ever.

O ye Fire and Heat, bless ye the Lord : praise him, and magnify him for ever.

O ye Winter and Summer, bless ye the Lord : praise him, and magnify him for ever.

O ye Dews and Frosts, bless ye the Lord : praise him, and magnify him for ever.

O ye Frost and Cold, bless ye the Lord : praise him, and magnify him for ever.

O ye Ice and Snow, bless ye the Lord : praise him, and magnify him for ever.

O ye Nights and Days, bless ye the Lord : praise him, and magnify him for ever.

O ye Light and Darkness, bless ye the Lord : praise him, and magnify him for ever.

O ye Lightnings and Clouds, bless ye the Lord : praise him, and magnify him for ever.

O let the Earth bless the Lord : yea, let it praise him, and magnify him for ever.

O ye Mountains and Hills, bless ye the Lord : praise him, and magnify him for ever.

O all ye Green Things upon the Earth, bless ye the Lord : praise him, and magnify him for ever.

O ye Wells, bless ye the Lord : praise him, and magnify him for ever.

O ye Seas and Floods, bless ye the Lord : praise him, and magnify him for ever.

O ye Whales, and all that move in the Waters, bless ye the Lord : praise him, and magnify him for ever.

O all ye Fowls of the Air, bless ye the Lord : praise him, and magnify him for ever.

O all ye Beasts and Cattle, bless ye the Lord : praise him, and magnify him for ever.

O ye Children of Men, bless ye the Lord : praise him, and magnify him for ever.

O let Israel bless the Lord : praise him, and magnify him for ever.

O ye Priests of the Lord, bless ye the Lord : praise him, and magnify him for ever.

O ye Servants of the Lord, bless ye the Lord : praise him, and magnify him for ever.

O ye Spirits and Souls of the Righteous, bless ye the Lord : praise him, and magnify him for ever.

O ye holy and humble Men of heart, bless ye the Lord : praise him, and magnify him for ever.

O Ananias, Azarias and Misael, bless ye the Lord : praise him, and magnify him for ever.

The Annunciation Window

22 January 2006
Readings: Isaiah 7:10–14; Luke 1:26–38

This sermon, on the Sin of Pride, was second in a series on the Seven Deadly Sins

In last week's sermon, our Chaplain spoke about how sermons on the Seven Deadly Sins were very much a fourteenth-century phenomenon, epitomised by Dante's *Divine Comedy*. Now I would never dare to argue with the Chaplain about the piety of the Middle Ages, given her doctoral studies on Julian of Norwich, but my own reading has made me wonder whether the numbering of seven for the Deadly Sins can be traced back much earlier than this – in fact, to biblical times. The seven oracles against the sins of seven foreign nations is a frequent feature in the prophets; and in the Gospels, Mary Magdalene has seven demons which need casting out; and the Apostle Paul offers a list of fourteen 'sins of the flesh' in Galatians 5. So the counting of sins, using the number seven (sometimes, intriguingly, seven plus one) was not unique to the Middle Ages, although it was clearly popularised then. It was a much earlier tradition.

Even by the fifth century, John Cassian, from southern Gaul, argued that Adam and Eve were guilty of all the Seven Deadly Sins when they took from the fruit of the Tree of Knowledge. A century or so later, Gregory the Great, writing from Rome, develops Cassian's ideas and lists the seven sins of Adam and Eve in order, starting with the spiritual and ending with the carnal. The Sin of Pride heads Gregory's list as the cardinal spiritual sin, out of which come Envy and Anger; and then, the carnal sins – Sloth, Covetousness, Gluttony and Lust. By the fourteenth century, Chaucer, in *The Parson's Tale*, similarly speaks of the 'barren tree of sin' which has its roots in Pride, and 'of this roote spryngen certain branches'. And as we heard last week, Dante, in *The Divine Comedy*, develops this view too: of the Seven Deadly Sins which are purged on their way to Purgatory, Pride comes first.

But medieval preaching and teaching did not just focus on vices and evils. The Books of Hours and the Morality Plays had a good deal to say about Christian virtues as well. Several lists of seven virtues 'offset' the seven sins – the seven petitions in the Lord's Prayer, the seven penitential psalms, the seven gifts of the spirit, the seven words from the cross, the seven wounds of Christ. The cardinal spiritual virtue underlying all these lists is Humility, for as Pride takes us far from God, Humility leads the sinner to repentance. Pride and Humility are actually two sides of the same coin: we overcome the Sin of Pride by the Grace of Humility, and we fail to achieve the Grace of Humility because we succumb to the Sin of Pride.

Given that this chapel was in part redesigned by William Burges to echo the visual art of the Middle Ages, it is not surprising to find that in this liturgical space we have several insights into this sevenfold theme. Clearly Burges enjoyed the number seven: the most obvious is the seven stained glass windows, in their different ways designed to show Christ as the Light of the World. Above the windows are the seven scrolls, showing how the narrative in the window was foretold in the Old Testament. Below the window are seven friezes – executed by Henry Holiday, who was also responsible in carrying out the designs for Burges' stained-glass windows. Each frieze serves a double purpose: in part it develops a theme in the window and in part it is a visual representation of parts of the Te Deum written out on the dado underneath. We shall return to these windows, scrolls and friezes shortly.

The antechapel takes up the theme of the number seven as well: here we find seven symbols of Judaism, representing what Burges saw as the 'old order', and when we walk into the chapel itself, we are invited to see how they have been fulfilled by the seven symbols of Christianity. The number seven is evident not only in the seven windows around the walls, but also, in a more subtle way, on the ceiling as well. On the ceiling, it is represented in the 'seven plus one' theme. In one medallion we see the four virtues taken from pagan sources (Justice, Perseverance, Purity and Moderation), and in the other, we see three virtues (Faith, Hope and Charity) taken from the teaching of Paul. An eighth, which is not in Paul's list, has been added to the seven to make eight in all: most appropriately for this sermon, the addition is the most important of all: this is the virtue of Humility.

The Four Christian Virtues: Faith, Hope, Charity and Humility.

In this series of sermons on the stained-glass windows in our Chapel, the obvious choice I intend to take tonight is the one which best illustrates the Grace of Humility overcoming the Sin of Pride. The window is on the north side of the chapel, nearest the door: it depicts the Annunciation by the angel Gabriel to Mary.

In the Middle Ages, Mary, as the epitome of the Grace of Humility, was often contrasted with Eve, the personification of the Sin of Pride. Interestingly, in our chapel this contrast between Mary

Eve expelled from the Garden.

The Epiphany Window.

The Window of Jesus in the Temple.

The East (Crucifixion) Window.

and Eve is evident as well, and one cannot help think that this was intentional.

Mary appears on four windows in the chapel: in this Annunciation Window, in the Epiphany Window directly opposite, in the window of Jesus in the Temple on the north side, and in the East Window which shows Mary at the foot of the cross. In each window we see her accepting the heavy burden of fulfilling the task of being 'theotokos', the mother of Jesus, Son of God. It is a task which brings her bewilderment and pain, and although all four windows are restrained in the way they portray this, we can see into her suffering nevertheless.

Eve appears twice in the chapel, both times on the ceiling. One is very close to the Crucifixion Window: this is Eve in the Garden of Eden, about to take the fruit of the Tree of Knowledge. Eve's desire to fulfil her own needs by eating the fruit of the tree could not be in a starker contrast to the suffering of Mary before the fruit of her body on the cross.

The second depiction of Eve is found closer to the Annunciation Window: indeed, high on the ceiling, it is actually midway between the Annunciation and Epiphany windows; there we see Eve and Adam being expelled from the Garden. Eve's Sin of Pride was that she loved herself more than she loved God; she had hoped the fruit would give her knowledge and power equal to his. If one looks up at Eve and then down to Mary, the contrast could not be more vivid: the horror and self-inflicted pain on Eve's face, and the quiet and dignified resignation to the will of God on Mary's. Here, in typical medieval typology, we have before us two different responses to God: the Sin of Pride and the Virtue of Humility. It seems to be no accident that Burges placed the two figures close together in order to make this important contrast clear.

Now let us focus just on the Annunciation Window itself. Burges' artist, Henry Holiday, has produced a design with a typically stylised account of the scene. Mary is sitting (usually she is either reading or sewing, in receptive mode: here she is reading, probably from a text in Isaiah, which fits with the scroll of Isaiah which is set above the window). The angel is behind her. The white lily

The scroll of the prophet Isaiah.

beside her serves as a symbol of purity – and death. The vines behind the angel are symbols of fecundity – and life. One motif in Annunciation scenes is often of a dove, symbolising the Holy Spirit: the dove is missing here, but the rose-hued colours of the angel's wings signify the cleansing power of the spirit. What is particularly unusual about this scene is that it seems to be set outside, rather than in Mary's house in Nazareth: did Burges intend to suggest that the promise of new life is made in another and different Garden from the one Adam and Eve had to leave?

Whether or not we are intended to look at Mary alongside Eve, what is clearly portrayed here is that this event was undoubtedly one of great portent. The scroll above the window makes this absolutely clear. The scroll has writing on it from the prophet Isaiah, whose prophecies occurred some eight hundred years earlier than the time of Mary. We heard the words on this scroll in our Old Testament lesson from Isaiah 9: 'Behold, a virgin shall conceive and bear a son, and he shall be called Immanuel, which means, God is with us'. So Mary, in the window below the scroll, apparently reading from the scroll by herself, is, by implication, identified as the 'virgin' spoken of by Isaiah; she is to be the one who will conceive and bear a son, who will become 'Immanuel', or 'God with us'. Isaiah's scroll and the Annunciation Window together reveal that this moment of encounter is no mere accident: it was prophesied long ago, and it is part of the great Divine Plan.

The problem with stylised representations, typical of medieval and renaissance art, is that the human aspects of this divine plan and angelic encounter prevent us from entering fully into the awesome consequences of Mary's response. Although the pain and grief are undoubtedly there, there is an element of stylised control. Mary remains an enigmatic, mysterious figure, passive, resigned; her inner struggle in attaining the gift of Humility is hinted at, but the agony and pain are not explicit.

For the more human details of Mary's sufferings we have to turn instead to the Gospel narrative which we heard earlier. There, in Luke chapter 1, we read that Mary was 'espoused' to Joseph: the usual age for such 'espousal' would probably have been between sixteen and eighteen. She is both vulnerable and innocent: the Annunciation Window has at least depicted something of this as Mary looks up at the angel. We also know that Joseph (who perhaps also deserves a sermon on the Grace of Humility) was known as a τέκτων ('tekton') in Greek – one skilled in wood and stone, a carpenter

The Annunciation Window and frieze under it.

and builder – perhaps what we would call a 'tradesman'. And from the sacrifice of just two pigeons that Mary and Joseph later made in the Temple as a thanksgiving for a safe birth, it is clear that Joseph's craft did not bring in much wealth. So her age, her social class, and even her relative poverty made her an extraordinary choice for one about to become the 'Mother of God'.

It was her physical vulnerability which resulted in her being able to become dependent upon God. Immediately after the Annunciation, Luke accords to Mary a song we hear sung every Sunday Evensong – the Magnificat. It illustrates so clearly Mary's response: God favours those of low estate, scattering the proud in the imagination of their hearts. 'He hath put down the mighty from their seats, and exalted them of low degree.' Here we can see how Mary's material poverty positively encouraged a spiritual poverty which enabled her to trust in God alone. Unlike Eve, the Grace of Humility was at work in her before her calling, rather than being a result of it, and it was this that equipped her for a lifetime of self-sacrificial love.

But does not this picture of Mary, materially as well as spiritually poor, make this an impossible goal for us to imitate? Our chapel window offers a part-answer to this. Look at the frieze under it, above the dado:

There you see various figures of authority in Church and State – a bishop, a priest, two monks, two nuns, a king, a queen, a noblewoman, a lawyer, an academic; some of them, it is argued, are represented as well-known

figures in and outside Oxford (King Olaf, it is argued, was remarkably similar to a then Fellow called Charles Henry Olive Daniel). It seems that in this frieze Burges invites us to enter the story of the Annunciation and the Magnificat: each of these figures, with their various gifts and vocations, different from each other and certainly from Mary, is shown as making their own choice of seeking that poverty of spirit which Mary exemplified.

And so we, the onlookers, each with our own various gifts and vocations – Provost, Chaplain, preacher, Fellows, lecturers, teachers, politicians, parents, graduates, scholars, undergraduates, sacristans, choirboys – we, the witnesses to this scene, whoever we are, whatever our calling, are given a similar challenge: to put aside self-esteem and self-aggrandisement and to pursue instead poverty of spirit whereby all that we are and all that we have is offered back to God.

We will often get it wrong. But even the greatest saints have recognized this. Saint Benedict – the spiritual father in whose name a chapel near this site was originally founded – in the seventh chapter of his Rule, speaks of humility as a ladder upon which we constantly ascend and descend. Our only hope is both to fear God and to know his love and understanding of us. Benedict is well aware that having achieved a small part of the Grace of Humility we then end up falling back into the Sin of Pride. But we should not give up. So as you walk out of Chapel tonight, under Adam and Eve expelled from the garden, and with Mary on your right, facing her challenge within that other garden, do look up at the words of a psalm which Burges has given us, above the West Door: 'Today if you will hear his voice, harden not your hearts'. And then remember Mary's response to God through the angel: 'Be it unto me according to your word'.

Appendix

Isaiah 7:10–14

[10] Again the LORD spoke to Ahaz, saying, [11] Ask a sign of the LORD your God; let it be deep as Sheol or high as heaven. [12] But Ahaz said, I will not ask, and I will not put the LORD to the test. [13] Then Isaiah said: "Hear then, O house of David! Is it too little for you to weary mortals, that you weary my God also? [14] Therefore the Lord himself will give you a sign. Look, the young woman is with child and shall bear a son, and shall name him Immanuel.

Luke 1:26–38

[26] In the sixth month the angel Gabriel was sent by God to a town in Galilee called Nazareth, [27] to a virgin engaged to a man whose name was Joseph, of the house of David. The virgin's name was Mary. [28] And he came to her and said, "Greetings, favored one! The Lord is with you." [29] But she was much perplexed by his words and pondered what sort of greeting this might be. [30] The angel said to her, "Do not be afraid, Mary, for you have found favour with God. [31] And now, you will conceive in your womb and bear a son, and you will name him Jesus. [32] He will be great, and will be called the Son of the Most High, and the Lord God will give to him the throne of his ancestor David. [33] He will reign over the house of Jacob forever, and of his kingdom there will be no end." [34] Mary said to the angel, "How can this be, since I am a virgin?" [35] The angel said to her, "The Holy Spirit will come upon you, and the power of the Most High will overshadow you; therefore the child to be born will be holy; he will be called Son of God. [36] And now, your relative Elizabeth in her old age has also conceived a son; and this is the sixth month for her who was said to be barren. [37] For nothing will be impossible with God." [38] Then Mary said, "Here am I, the servant of the Lord; let it be with me according to your word." Then the angel departed from her.

The Epiphany Window

6 November 2006 (Feast of Christ the King)
There were six lessons and carols; Matthew 2:1–12 preceded the sermon

This sermon was given at the College Advent Carol Service

You might have been wondering where the stained-glass window on the front of your Advent Service Sheet is from. The windows are not easy to see at Evensong at this time of year, as they were designed with a morning congregation more in mind, but the image is actually one of our chapel's windows – the one on the right of the door as you come in. I have been giving a series of sermons on all seven windows, and this one fits well with the theme of our service tonight.

William Burges, the architect responsible for the refurbishment of this chapel in the 1860s (you can see the date of its completion on the ceiling as you go out) was a Victorian who believed passionately in the power of the visual to communicate profound spiritual truths. So he covered the walls, ceilings, floors and furniture with people and themes from the Bible, church history, the classical tradition and the natural world, whilst his glazier, Henry Holiday, applied his skills to Burges' plans for the windows, on the theme of 'Christ the Light of the World'. You only have to look briefly round this chapel to see how rich it is in many different sorts of symbolism. Burges allowed these illustrations to serve as a commentary on the theological and social issues of his day. For example, the decorations around the windows can be seen to reflect the debates about Darwinism and Creation; whereas the ceilings and the antechapel echo other nineteenth-century controversies about the relationship between Jews and Christians. And on the floor, behind the altar, and in the windows, we find nineteenth-century allusions to the disputes about the role of the church in society. In the 1860s, undergraduates and Fellows alike would have had to attend chapel daily, usually for morning prayer, so there was plenty of opportunity for reflection and debate on these things. Some one hundred and fifty years later, when we so rarely come to chapel except for special occasions such as this, we have lost much of this interaction; and that is why I am trying to revive some of it in this series of sermons.

So I want to focus tonight on what is called the Epiphany Window, which speaks of the 'epiphany', or 'manifestation', of the Christ-Child to the Three Kings. It is a story, along with other stories of the Nativity, which has been frequently repeated in the great medieval cathedral windows of northern France and England. Burges was concerned to bring medieval art and architecture into nineteenth-century public and private spaces, and in this chapel he did it with great attention to detail. However, in this particular window he also did something rather different, because, despite its medieval associations, he gave it a nineteenth-century political spin. In this stylised contemporary commentary on the visit of the Three Kings, we see something which reflects particular British interests – concerns about the nature of monarchies and the extent of their powers, a topic which was both topical and contentious in the latter part of the nineteenth century when the chapel was refurbished.

Take a closer look at the stylised details of this window. There is no stable, no ox and ass; and instead of looking into a nativity scene, we find ourselves looking outwards, from the entrance of a house. You can see the portico, the silhouettes of the trees against the darkened sky, and the star casting its piercing shaft of light – almost like a sword – onto the Virgin and Child. And when we look at the visitors, it is quite clear that they are not magi or astrologers from the East, in traditional Oriental garb, but rather rulers of the kingdoms from the Western Christendom. Admittedly, the third figure in the background has a turban, but even he seems to typify the kingdom of the Turks – itself a relevant topic given the Crimean War just a few years earlier. And the clothes of the other two – the one in red presenting myrrh, the one in gold and silver offering his golden crown – are distinctly Anglo-Saxon in physique and dress. The blue and black canopy, in the top left of the window, is embossed with more modern royal symbols, and it protects the Virgin Mary, who in turn protects her baby son and holds a serene and regal pose. The infant Jesus, supported by Mary, resting on a purple pillow, looks upwards and outwards: although only a few weeks old, he possesses a wisdom and composure way beyond his years. And we, as spectators, are included in this scene; together we can observe the contrast between the rulers who hold earthly but temporal power and the simple authority of the Christ-Child, whose kingdom we, the audience, now know in the hindsight of his life and death was in this world but not of it.

Most of the details of this scene are taken from Matthew's Gospel, and follow the reading we heard a few minutes ago. Matthew says nothing about a stable; he is similarly silent about any ox and ass; there are no angels, no visit of the shepherds: all those details are in Luke's Gospel. Matthew sets this scene some time after Jesus' birth, still in Bethlehem, but this time in a house, not in Luke's stable. So up to this point the window is true to the account in Matthew. However, in Matthew, as we heard, the visitors are described as 'magi' – astrologers, following signs and portents through a star – not kings. Yet despite this, the kingship theme is undoubtedly a sub-theme in Matthew's story, and this is what Burges has developed more explicitly in this window. In Matthew we read of these magi first enquiring of Herod, the Hasmonean King in nearby Jerusalem, as to the whereabouts of the 'one born King of the Jews'. This innocent encounter arouses the jealousy of king Herod; and when he discovers that the child has been born in Bethlehem, the ancient birthplace of the great Jewish king, David, the city where many believed the promised 'King of the Jews' would be born, Herod's jealousy spills over to murder. When the magi leave the country, he routs out and kills all potential infant rivals to his throne. Matthew's account has undoubtedly been influenced by the debates about the nature of kingship in first century Judea, and this is the theme which Burges, too, has chosen to develop more explicitly.

So what we see here is the 'kings of this world' – in its nineteenth-century setting, probably from the kingdoms of Europe – paying homage to a baby whom they only partially understand has a kingdom which surpasses theirs. It is a bizarre sight: those who hold power give it back to one who, in all the vulnerability of birthing and infancy, is utterly powerless. That this is what Burges intended is evident in what he has placed above the window and below it. If you look up above the window you will see a scroll held by the prophet Zechariah. Each window has its own caption through a prophet holding an unfurled scroll; and the one over this particular window is taken from Zechariah 14:9: 'And the Lord will become king over all the earth'.

The theme of 'Christ the King' has been a golden thread running throughout our service tonight, and given that we are starting the season of Advent, it is most apposite. We encountered it in our very first hymn, 'Once in royal David's city', where we sang of Jesus' first coming as a baby, and his

The scroll of the prophet Zechariah.

second coming as King over all the earth. We came across the theme again as we prayed the Lord's Prayer: 'Thy kingdom come… for thine is the kingdom, the power and the glory…'. We heard it in the earlier reading from Isaiah 9, which spoke about one who was to be born from the house of David and who would bring in the rule of God. And in the hymn 'O little town of Bethlehem', we sang of how 'the hopes and fears of all the years' have been met in the birth of this child.

The idea of a 'child born to be king' and the idea of a kingdom 'in but not of this world' is an intriguing one; it speaks of the 'upside-down' nature of the Christian Gospel, where 'Christ the Light of the World' confounds human expectations of what a redeeming figure should be like. Burges has explored in it at least two other windows. One is the window directly opposite, of Mary and the angel Gabriel, which, as we heard in an earlier reading, speaks of God confounding the mighty and powerful and rich and choosing the meek and powerless through whom to bring about his work of salvation. The most vivid illustration of this reversal of power and powerlessness is in the Crucifixion Window above the altar: here we see Christ, the 'King of the Jews', who, having refuted worldly power, effects salvation by being as vulnerable in his death as he was in his birth. The title over his cross is in fact, again, 'King of the Jews': it links together his birth and his death and shows us how the one who was born to be a different sort of king – for us – also dies as a different sort of king – for us. T.S. Eliot, in his poem 'The Journey of the Magi', also dwells on this theme as it relates to our own window. In the words of one of the magi, having returned to his land from that visit to Bethlehem, we hear:

Were we led all that way for
Birth or Death? There was a Birth, certainly,
We have evidence and no doubt. I have seen birth and death
But had thought they were different; this Birth was
Hard and bitter agony for us, like Death, our death.
We returned to our places, these Kingdoms,
But no longer at ease here, in the old dispensation,
With an alien people clutching their gods.
I should be glad of another death.

Burges developed this 'reversal' theme not only in the scroll above the window but in the frieze below it. Each window has its own scroll as textual commentary, and its own frieze as a visual commentary, and the frieze takes up the theme yet further.

The frieze is of well-known saints and martyrs of the Christian Church: Burges' comments on his own designs reveal that these are of Stephen, the first martyr of the Christian Church, then Polycarp, one of the first bishops of the Church to die a martyr, then Thomas Becket, martyred for his faith in Canterbury Cathedral, then Catherine, a fourth-century martyr who was killed by being fastened to a wheel, then Perpetua, a third-century martyr from North Africa, then Cecilia, a second-century martyr who died singing praises to God (as the patron saint of music she is represented here with her pipes). Also represented here are Jan Huss, a fourteenth-century Bohemian martyr, and another fourteenth-century martyr, Jerome of Prague. Lastly are two sixteenth-century English martyrs, Latimer and Hooper – each in their time bishops of Worcester. This is a parade of those who have each renounced the love of power, and who have voluntarily laid down their lives for the kingdom of God, drawn by the power of love. They, in effect, carry out in practice what the Three Kings in the window above have learned in principle. The kings had yet to learn that they would serve their cause best when they recognised the temporal and temporary nature of their calling. The martyrs, by contrast, accepting the temporary and temporal powers of this world, not only set their eyes on Christ the King but also gave up their lives for a kingdom which would last forever.

Below and opposite: A frieze of Christian martyrs.

So where does that leave us, as we look through the window to what lies beyond? We are neither kings nor martyrs; but our response can be simple yet profound as we are moved to make our own homage. In the words of the carol by Christina Rossetti which we heard the choir sing so movingly earlier:

> *What can I give Him,*
> *Poor as I am?*
> *If I were a shepherd,*
> *I would bring a lamb,*
> *If I were a wise man,*
> *I would do my part.*
> *Yet what I can I give Him*
> *Give my heart.*

This is surely a small token to offer the one whose purpose in coming into this world was to demonstrate, again and again, *the power of love* over and above *the love of power.*

Appendix:
Matthew 2:1–12

[1] In the time of King Herod, after Jesus was born in Bethlehem of Judea, wise men from the East came to Jerusalem, [2] asking, "Where is the child who has been born king of the Jews? For we observed his star at its rising, and have come to pay him homage." [3] When King Herod heard this, he was frightened, and all Jerusalem with him; [4] and calling together all the chief priests and scribes of the people, he inquired of them where the Messiah was to be born. [5] They told him, "In Bethlehem of Judea; for so it has been written by the prophet: [6] 'And you, Bethlehem, in the land of Judah, are by no means least among the rulers of Judah; for from you shall come a ruler who is to shepherd my people of Israel.'" [7] Then Herod secretly called for the wise men and learned from them the exact time when the star had appeared. [8] Then he sent them to Bethlehem, saying, "Go and search diligently for the child; and when you have found him, bring

me word so that I may also go and pay him homage." [9] When they had heard the king, they set out; and there, ahead of them, went the star that they had seen at its rising, until it stopped over the place where the child was. [10] When they saw that the star had stopped, they were overwhelmed with joy. [11] On entering the house, they saw the child with Mary his mother; and they knelt down and paid him homage. Then, opening their treasure chests, they offered him gifts of gold, frankincense, and myrrh. [12] And having been warned in a dream not to return to Herod, they left for their own country by another road.

The Window of the Presentation of Christ in the Temple

7 November 2004
Readings: Malachi 3: 1–4; Luke 2: 40–52

This sermon was given at the Presentation of the Scholars in the Chapel

When in the mid-nineteenth century William Burges refurbished this chapel, he left intact the structure created by the eighteenth-century architect, James Wyatt, and instead filled up every available space – the niches, ceilings, floors, windows and walls – with visual imagery. Wyatt's edifice, with its pilasters and ionic columns, gave the chapel the appearance of a classical Greek temple. Burges adopted and expanded the idea. The chapel was still to echo Greek classical models, but it was to be enriched by a Jewish-Christian schema as well. In the antechapel, Burges developed the Hellenistic influence by frescos which echoed designs taken from Pompeii and Herculaneum; but also in this space he added specifically Jewish designs to make the entry look like the Tent of Meeting – a portable shrine used by the Israelite people before the building of Solomon's Temple – replete with representations of the Ark, the Scrolls of Law and the Seven-Branched Candlestick, for example.

The scrolls of the Law.

Burges did the same in the chapel itself. There he preserved the pillars and the dome to continue the impression of 'Temple architecture', but on the domed ceiling he combined, near the entrance, images of four classical virtues (these surround the fresco of Adam and Eve being banished from the Garden) with, near the altar, four Judaic-Christian ones (these encompass the fresco of Adam and Eve taking the fruit from the tree in the midst of the Garden). The architectural impression of the chapel as a whole is of the outer court (the antechapel), the inner court (the nave) and holy of holies (the chancel) – a design which is associated both with pagan and Jewish temples.

So you are sitting here in what could be both a Greek and Jewish temple, in a tradition which is both classical and biblical. This is a place where you can encounter both the God of the Judaic-Christian tradition and commune with the God of Nature as well. The chapel's liturgy flows naturally out of both these traditions.

I want us to focus on one example of this 'Temple tradition'. It's depicted in one of the chapel windows – the one in the middle of the north side (or to your left as you stand facing the altar) – and its theme is the Presentation of Christ in the Temple. It depicts the boy Jesus at the Temple in Jerusalem: our New Testament reading from Luke was an account of it.

Henry Holiday, the glazier who carried out Burges' designs for this window, has represented the boy Jesus as any adolescent – he could be just another choirboy. He is clearly engaged in some debate with the religious leaders; the scroll in his hand, and the jar, full of scrolls by the seated priest, indicates that this 'tutorial essay' is going to extend well beyond its appointed time. Above this scene, Holiday has depicted – rather oddly – Mary and Joseph walking in the

The Seven-Branched Candlestick.

Temple architecture from the West Door and East Window

opposite direction, apparently unable to see their son because they're walking behind the colonnade, but their faces and posture clearly reveal their concern about his whereabouts, and their obliviousness to his presence in the Temple.

I'm not asserting that, in aesthetic terms, this Pre-Raphaelite-influenced window has the same vibrancy of earlier masters who have painted the same scene: one image I have is of Veronese's painting, in the Museo del Prado, Madrid, where Jesus is standing on some steps against a pillar of the Temple, declaiming passionately in a way which foreshadows his *cleansing* of the Temple some fifteen years later. Our Worcester window, admittedly, has a less dramatic and artistic appeal. But Holiday's depiction of this youthful, innocent Jesus, engrossed in learning rather than teaching, is an important facet of Jesus in his humility rather than his authority and power. The placing of his anxious parents at the back of the scene symbolises Jesus' youthful dependency on them: the seeds of his divine nature are just beginning to flower in his engagement with the Jewish teachers, but they are certainly not yet in full bloom.

Above each of these seven windows, Burges set an Old Testament text, in order to show how the words spoken by seven typical Old Testament prophets were in the process of being fulfilled in seven typical scenes in the life of Christ. The text above this 'Presentation' window was read earlier: it is from Malachi, and it speaks of the Lord 'suddenly coming to his Temple'. Malachi, like all the other prophetic figures above the windows, is holding a partially furled scroll, indicating by its semi-closure that the full significance of his words have yet to be fulfilled. There are just enough words visible to know this is from a verse which reads '*The Lord whom you seek will suddenly come to the Temple*'.

This is not the place to deliver a lecture on the place of the Temple in the Bible, but suffice it to say that it is a major theme throughout the Old and New Testaments. In Old Testament tradition, the Temple is where God dwells in one unique and special place, a prototype of a more focused

The scroll of the prophet Malachi.

incarnation amongst his people, protecting and guiding them throughout political and religious crises. The First Temple was built by Solomon in the tenth century BCE, but was razed to the ground by the Babylonians some four hundred years later; the Second Temple was rebuilt with the financial help of the kings of Persia some eighty years after that, but it was a disappointing edifice in many ways, and made the people constantly yearn for something greater, when, independent of foreign control, they would see God return to his people in all his glory. This is what the prophet Malachi, the last of the prophets of the Hebrew Bible, is implying when, aware of the flagging faith of the Jewish community in Jerusalem, he says 'the Lord, whom you seek, will suddenly come to his Temple'.

Those who have some knowledge of the Gospels may recall other occasions when Jesus 'suddenly comes to the Temple'. The first was as a baby, when, according to Jewish law, as the first-born son of Mary and Joseph, he had to be presented before the Jerusalem priests: the only sacrifice which his parents could afford was of a pair of turtle doves or two pigeons. In this meagre offering, Mary and Joseph were dedicating their son back to God – ironically not realising the full significance of what they were doing. The second time Jesus comes to the Temple is depicted in this window here. The third occasion was when he drove out the moneychangers from the Temple – a dramatic illustration of the challenge of his authority over the priests and scribes regarding the interpretation of the Jewish Law and the Jewish Messiah, for on this occasion he called the Temple 'my father's house'. The fourth time was on the night before he died, when he was tried for blasphemy – claiming equality to God; he was tried in the house of Caiaphas the high priest, whose living quarters were close to the Temple. This last episode is narrated with some irony: who, in actual fact, is judging whom?

On each occasion when Jesus comes to the Temple, Malachi's prophecy is radically reused. Earlier in his life, rather than taking on the assumed mantle of power and glory, Jesus appears first in poverty, as a baby, and then in vulnerability, as a boy. His other two appearances, shortly before his crucifixion, may express more authority, but they hardly fulfilled the Jewish expectations popularised by prophets such as Malachi about God suddenly coming to his Temple in power and glory. The debate with the Jewish authorities, which began when Jesus was about twelve and continued until his early death, was, in essence, about where true wisdom could be found – whether, in traditional Jewish teaching, in the authority of the Jewish Law and the teaching about the

Opposite and right: Twelve prophetic figures from the Old Testament and (far right) two from the New.

Messiah, or whether, according to Jesus, in God incarnate through his person, speaking and working *beyond* the confines of the Temple.

It would not have taken much insight for the Jews of Jesus' day to associate these instances of his being in the Temple with the prophecy of Malachi. But, typical of the stylised way Burges organised all seven windows, he also allows further visual commentary in the frieze which is below it. This depicts twelve very different 'prophets' who in various ways were concerned about God's presence with his people, especially in the Temple. Taken as a group, they serve to reinforce the authority of Malachi and his words about God 'suddenly appearing in the Temple'.

Burges informs us in his various comments on the chapel that he included Enoch, Noah, and a prophetess, called Miriam in this iconography – all prophets spoken of in the Torah. He then depicts David, who captured Jerusalem and laid the foundations of the Temple; then Solomon, his son, who is holding a model of the Temple; then Huldah, a prophetess who was consulted about reforming Temple worship. Then, as representations from the prophetic books, we have Isaiah, Daniel, and Malachi, all of whom are connected in different ways with prophecies of hope about God returning to his people and to the Temple. The last two 'prophets' in this frieze are from the New Testament – John the Baptist and Anna. As a miscellany of twelve, they reinforce the prophetic words of the scroll above – that the Lord *will* suddenly return to his Temple; and as they reiterate the prophet's words, they also direct our eyes back to the window, when we have to see that, in a totally unexpected way, their messages are now in the process of being fulfilled.

This may seem rather complicated and dense theology, but I believe it could nevertheless have a great deal of relevance for those who've come to Chapel today, perhaps for the first time, to have your scholarship ratified by our rather quaint and ancient College traditions. The chapel context,

your scholars' gowns, even the Latin medium of your promises, are all symbols of a long continuity with the College's history, of which you now play a special part. This brief ceremony draws its inspiration from the motto of the University – *Dominus illuminatio mea* – 'The *Lord* is my Light', and is intended to suggest that the skills of learning and the talents of understanding are *gifts*, not rights; so, as gifts, they deserve to be handed over back to God the Giver. In Christian terms, there is nothing new in the idea of handing back one's gifts and skills to God: it takes us back to the Benedictine foundation of the College, and its fundamental belief that *study* and *prayer* were two sides of the same coin; it's depicted in the frieze at the back of the altar, where, on the north side, the Benedictine monk is offering the College itself (literally, by way of a model!), back to God, and on the south side, Thomas Cookes is doing the same.

Hence tonight could be a presentation of your own skills and gifts back to God, in Burges' pseudo-Greek, pseudo-Jewish 'Temple-Chapel'. It could be a way of you indicating your willingness, like the young Jesus, to enter a tutorial-type debate with the Christian Church about where true wisdom is to be found. Burges' twofold Temple symbolism at least gives a choice. You may well prefer the more naturalist, human-centred, rationalist legacy of the Enlightenment, assuming, in ways not dissimilar from our Greek forebears, that human wisdom and knowledge are skills to be prized, not gifts to be offered back to God; the Greek Temple idea may therefore be your model, and the presence of Christ within it may be a bit of an encumbrance. But I urge you at least to *consider* the other model, in line with the Judaic-Christian tradition, that your intellect is a gift, not a right, and that the giver is, in fact, the God and Father of Jesus Christ. Burges was pretty astute in offering us, architecturally, a Greek model of σοφία (the Greek word for wisdom) which is primarily a model of self-sufficient knowledge, and a Jewish-Christian model of חָכְמָה (the Hebrew word 'hokmah') which is about God-given wisdom. The choice is yours, but its implications on the way you do your study are enormous.

These stained-glass windows, especially the one of the presence of Christ in the Temple, remind me of words from George Herbert's collection of lyric poems in *The Temple*. A verse from the poem 'The Elixir' is most pertinent:

> *A man that looks on glass,*
> *On it may stay his eye,*
> *Or, if he pleaseth, through it pass,*
> *And then the heav'n espy.*

Appendix

Malachi 3:1–4

[1] See, I am sending my messenger to prepare the way before me, and the Lord whom you seek will suddenly come to his temple. The messenger of the covenant in whom you delight – indeed, he is coming, says the LORD of hosts. [2] But who can endure the day of his coming, and who can stand when he appears? For he is like a refiner's fire and like fullers' soap; [3] he will sit as a refiner and purifier of silver, and he will purify the descendants of Levi and refine them like gold and silver, until they present offerings to the LORD in righteousness. [4] Then the offering of Judah and Jerusalem will be pleasing to the LORD as in the days of old and as in former years.

Luke 2:40 – 52

[40] The child grew and became strong, filled with wisdom; and the favor of God was upon him. [41] Now every year his parents went to Jerusalem for the festival of the Passover. [42] And when he was twelve years old, they went up as usual for the festival. [43] When the festival was ended and they started to return, the boy Jesus stayed behind in Jerusalem, but his parents did not know it. [44] Assuming that he was in the group of travelers, they went a day's journey. Then they started to look for him among their relatives and friends. [45] When they did not find him, they returned to Jerusalem to search for him. [46] After three days they found him in the temple, sitting among the teachers, listening to them and asking them questions. [47] And all who heard him were amazed at his understanding and his answers. [48] When his parents saw him they were astonished; and his mother said to him, "Child, why have you treated us like this? Look, your father and I have been searching for you in great anxiety." [49] He said to them, "Why were you searching for me? Did you not know that I must be in my Father's house?" [50] But they did not understand what he said to them. [51] Then he went down with them and came to Nazareth, and was obedient to them. His mother treasured all these things in her heart. [52] And Jesus increased in wisdom and in years, and in divine and human favour.

The Baptism Window

29 May 2005
Readings: Joel 2:27–29; Mark 1:1–11

It is a shame that we do not have more baptisms here in the chapel. Four weeks ago the Chaplain's little daughter was baptised here, amidst a cluster of soft toys and toddlers and babies on the marble floor: it was wonderful to have some informality and humanity in this liturgical space, and Katherine Eleanor Pennington rose to the challenge with impeccable good manners. It was a moving occasion. Would that this sermon on the Baptism Window could be in the context of a baptism service! However, whether we have been baptised or not, there are several insights we can all take from a closer look at this window.

Each of the seven windows has been organised around the theme of 'Christ the Light of the World', and each has been given an identical structure. First, all seven have been placed with a wall panel on either side, which testify, by contrast, to God as Creator of the world. Then, high above each window – actually above the dado – there is a partly furled scroll on which is written a commentary on the window from some Old Testament prophet, in order to show how the event recorded in the window is a deliberate fulfilment of Jewish hope and faith. And underneath each window there is a gilt-coloured frieze of different groups of Christians – in the case of the Baptism Window, the group is of the apostles – which add a human commentary on the theological theme in the window. So although the windows are the focal point in these sermons, it is important to take in as well the other parts of this deliberately stylised design.

The Baptism Window was originally intended to be placed where the Annunciation Window (the one next to it, towards the door) is now. The architect, William Burges, had thought the order should be, on the south side, the three critical events in Jesus' adult life which testified to his being the Son of God – the Baptism, the Empty Tomb and the Ascension. By contrast, Burges had intended the north side to represent the three critical events in Jesus' birth and childhood which pointed to his divine origins – the Annunciation, the Visit of the Three Kings and the boy Jesus in the Temple. But Burges changed this order, probably because he wanted us to look at the windows not down the one side of the chapel and then the other, but more chronologically as we come in. So as we enter we have the Annunciation on our left and the Epiphany on our right; we then have the boy Jesus in the Temple on our left and opposite it the Baptism; then the Empty Tomb is on our left, and opposite it, the Ascension. The Crucifixion east window broods over the other six and in effect dominates them.

Whatever we might make of these windows theologically, they certainly illustrate that blend of thirteenth-century High Gothic and nineteenth-century High Victorian iconography which Burges and his glazier Holiday loved. Their aesthetic appeal is in the eye of the beholder: but they were clearly intended to open up to the viewer aspects of another, theological world.

One interesting theological comment is the way the Baptism Window is set within the context of the Creation wall panels on each side of it. In this case the panels are in praise of God as Creator of the seas and floods. The theme of the power of the mighty waters is used to highlight the motif of Jesus' cleansing in the river Jordan and to give the scene a broader Creation orientation: God who brings about creation through the separation of the salt waters and fresh waters is the same God who brings about a new creation in individuals through the purging waters of baptism. By bringing together the theme of God the Creator in the wall panels and God the Redeemer in the window itself, the sacrament of baptism is given a more profound context: those who are given physical life through God's act of creation and spiritual life through God's gift of baptism are, as it were, twice held within the grace of God.

The scroll high above this scene offers a different sort of commentary altogether. The words are from the prophet Joel and read, 'I will pour my spirit upon all flesh': this was the text we had for our Old Testament reading tonight. Although Burges could have chosen many other Old Testament passages about water and cleansing, he chose this one to emphasise the part that the Spirit plays in a person's baptism, beginning with Jesus himself. So the window shows Jesus being anointed with the Spirit as a way of announcing the beginning of his public ministry, and the transforming power of the Spirit is symbolised by the purity and gentleness of a dove. The dove might seem an odd symbol of the Spirit; but it takes us back again to the theme of creation, when at the very beginning of Genesis the Spirit of God hovers like a great bird over the primordial waters, bringing order into the formlessness and void. It also reminds us of the Flood story later on in Genesis, when the return of the dove to the Ark is an announcement that the waters were beginning to abate, and God's recreation of his world is about to begin. So the scroll and the symbolism of the Spirit as a dove again reminds us that the Spirit of God the Creator and the Spirit of God the Redeemer are one and the same, bringing order into our lives instead of chaos and giving the promise of new beginnings, both physical and spiritual.

Before we look at how the lower frieze of the apostles fits in with this, we need to focus a little more on the window itself. In its distinctive Pre-Raphaelite way, it evokes some of the scene which our reading from Mark's Gospel described. John the Baptist stands on the banks of the river Jordan: he is

The theme of water in the side panels and the Baptism Window.

The scroll of the prophet Joel.

clothed, as Mark describes, in 'camel's hair with a girdle of skin about his loins'. Jesus, in John's own words, was 'mightier than I', is depicted as submitting himself to John's baptism as he stands below him in the water, demonstrating the same meekness and identification with humanity, which was the hallmark of his adult ministry, right up to his death. Mark informs us that the descent of the Spirit 'like a dove' was accompanied by a voice from heaven, affirming Jesus as God's Son by quoting a verse from a psalm: 'Thou art my beloved Son, in whom I am well pleased'. The window seems to capture that moment when both baptiser and baptised hear this voice: John looks up to heaven, and Jesus looks up to John. So Jesus' baptism marks the inauguration of his earthly ministry – it shows how it is to be one of humble service and of intimacy with God.

If we look more closely at Jesus' gaze at John, we may also note a contrast between the two cousins. John could only baptise with water, but Jesus, having received the Spirit, will also baptise by the Spirit. The dove symbolises not only the Holy Spirit given *to* Jesus but the same Spirit soon to be given *by* Jesus to all those who respond to his call to join the Kingdom of God. Unlike John's baptism by water, Jesus' baptism with the Spirit is therefore to be an inner as well as outer cleansing. The greenness of the setting – the grasses, the bulrushes, the foliage on the trees and the fields and hills behind – shows us that, unlike all the other scenes recorded on these seven windows, we are in the country, away from the pressures of Bethlehem or Jerusalem or Nazareth, and the lushness of the place and the freshness of creation marks new life and new beginnings. Burges undoubtedly took artistic liberty in making this scene part of the English countryside, well watered and verdant with the richness of nature which he so loved. This is of course something we can readily identify with. It brings Jesus into 'England's green and pleasant land'.

In most of the windows I rather like the way in which Burges has brought an old but familiar story into a nineteenth-century setting. But with this particular window, I just wonder if Burges has missed an important point in the original account. For although it undoubtedly brings Jesus' baptism closer to home in our own verdant land, it nevertheless domesticates this event and compromises its meaning.

I am aware that some of you – Worcester theologians, for example – have actually been to the river Jordan at the point where it enters the city of Jericho. You will probably remember how humid and airless it is there: it is close to the lowest point on the Earth's surface. And although there *is* some evidence of vegetation and palm trees, signifying signs of water nearby, the surrounding panorama is actually pretty arid; and the need for a cool drink or douse of water is fairly intense. There are distant hills which signify the place in the desert associated with the temptations of Christ (an event which immediately followed the baptism), and, turning south, the desert landscape falls into the Dead Sea, with its various austere, isolated Jewish settlements, like those in which John the Baptist may well have temporarily lived.

So Jesus' baptism was by no means the wonderfully refreshing scene which this window implies. In its original setting on the banks of the Jordan, the impression would have been of the healing restorative power of water, but in the context of heat, aridity and dehydration. The water of the river Jordan, with the desert so close at hand, is hardly a commodity to take for granted; the waters symbolise rather vividly a quenching of thirst and a rare opportunity for cleansing, suggesting God's provision of our needs when we are at our most parched and most needy.

This rather subdued take on the Baptism certainly makes sense of the frieze beneath the window. Represented there is the company of the twelve apostles – Peter with his key to the Church, and Andrew with his cross, for example. We know nothing of when the apostles were baptised, nor even whether it was by Jesus himself during his lifetime. But we do know that as a result of their commitment to him they knew more about the heat of the desert and the need to be utterly dependent on God's provision than the delights of a riverside scene and the advantages of a life which was verdant and luxurious. We have retained this idea in the baptism service today by offering the one baptised the mark of the cross; this is a reminder that to be baptised is to belong to the community of all those others who also bear the mark of the cross, and that bearing that mark is not about choosing an easy life, but rather one with hardship and suffering, following the mark of the cross in the shadow of their Master.

So this Baptism Window is witness to two paradoxical aspects of the Christian life. On the one hand, it offers us assurance that the God of Creation – the one who upholds all the Created Order – is the same omnipotent and transcendent God who meets us when we seek to identify with the person and work of Christ, and he is capable of sustaining us with his Spirit when our resources are low. On the other hand, it offers us the challenge that if we wish to follow Christ, we will inevitably find that

we have to face some of the suffering and outrage he had to face. In short, being baptised is not only about receiving resources from God but also about giving our own resources back to him.

In the end, I rather like this window. It glamorises and romanticises the act of baptism, showing it to be more about what we might receive than what we might have to give. But because of the frieze beneath, it also reminds us that the resources of baptism inevitably lead us on to understanding the demands it makes on us as well. So whether baptised or not, I hope that when you return to chapel and look up at this Baptism Window you will at least reflect upon what God in Christ is prepared to do for you and with you; and if you allow yourself to be humbled before God, as Jesus did before John, this will allow God's Spirit to work in you and through you.

Appendix
Joel 2:27–29

27 You shall know that I am in the midst of Israel, and that I, the LORD, am your God and there is no other. And my people shall never again be put to shame. 28 Then afterward I will pour out my spirit on all flesh; your sons and your daughters shall prophesy, your old men shall dream dreams, and your young men shall see visions. 29 Even on the male and female slaves, in those days, I will pour out my spirit.

Mark 1:1–11

1 The beginning of the good news of Jesus Christ, the Son of God. 2 As it is written in the prophet Isaiah, "See, I am sending my messenger ahead of you, who will prepare your way; 3 the voice of one crying out in the wilderness: 'Prepare the way of the Lord, make his paths straight,'" 4 John the baptiser appeared in the wilderness, proclaiming a baptism of repentance for the forgiveness of sins. 5 And people from the whole Judean countryside and all the people of Jerusalem were going out to him, and were baptised by him in the river Jordan, confessing their sins. 6 Now John was clothed with camel's hair, with a leather belt around his waist, and he ate locusts and wild honey. 7 He proclaimed, "The one who is more powerful than I is coming after me; I am not worthy to stoop down and untie the thong of his sandals. 8 I have baptised you with water; but he will baptise you with the Holy Spirit." 9 In those days Jesus came from Nazareth of Galilee and was baptised by John in the Jordan. 10 And just as he was coming up out of the water, he saw the heavens torn apart and the Spirit descending like a dove on him. 11 And a voice came from heaven, "You are my Son, the Beloved; with you I am well pleased."

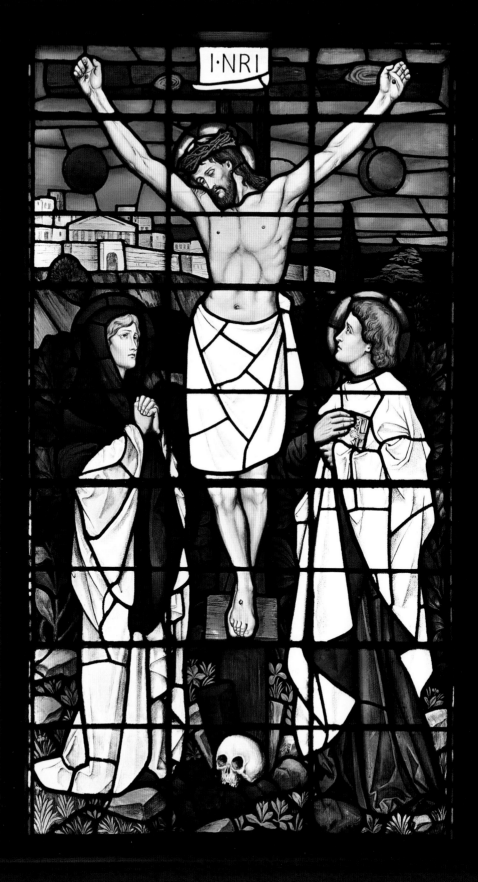

The Crucifixion Window

Remembrance Sunday, 13 November 2005
Readings: Daniel 9:24–27; John 19: 16–30

It is more than likely that several of you here will know someone who has had senile dementia. It is a dreadful thing. I too know a little about this, as my mother suffers from it, and each time we visit her, the symptoms are increasingly evident. Her short-term memory loss means that she often cannot remember where she is or why she is where she is, or indeed why we have come or where we have come from, let alone what day it is or what her grandchildren are called. Yet her long-term memory is quite another matter; given the right occasion, she has been able to recall quite well the war years when she worked as an ambulance driver for Leeds General Hospital.

It seems that we who never experienced the world wars have a curious reversal of memory loss. Our short-term memories are still sharp – as life gets increasingly busy, we have to concentrate, often simultaneously, on the immediate past, present and future; but our long-term memories can sometimes be more deficient. And when it comes to remembering war, I would think that most of you have no memory even of the Falklands War: your first real memories must have been of the 1990 Gulf War.

'At the going down of the sun and in the morning we will remember them'. Yet, without informed memory, how can we remember what we do not know? For those of us born after World War Two our act of remembering has to be through a deliberate act of creative imagination. The process of recalling the past, even a past we may never have in experience known, is vital for our own well-being; otherwise we shall take for granted the freedom those who fought for us have given to us, and we will then lose all compassion, assuming that the privilege of living in a free world is in fact our right.

One of my own most stirring memories was a visit to Yad Veshem, the Holocaust Museum, in Jerusalem, where imagining the intense pain of the *Shoah* and the concentration camps was simply horrific. Others among you will have different associations. For some it is likely to be a visit to the battlefields of the two world wars, whether the beaches of Normandy, or the valley of the Somme, Passchendaele and Flanders Fields, where, in John McCrae's words,

> ... *the poppies blow*
> *Between the crosses, row on row*
> *That mark our place; and in the sky*
> *The larks, still bravely singing fly*
> *Scarce heard amid the guns below.*

For others it may be an image of a war cemetery – those interminable rows of crosses, as faceless as the names of our alumni which we heard read out tonight – where even in the anonymity, we intuit some pain as we realise each was somebody's lover, somebody's child. Another evocation, not far from here, is the painting in the Lodgings – many of you must have seen it on your way in to Collections – which was completed in 1937, of some seventeen undergraduates in the Cloisters, enjoying college life – music, drama, sport, work, and simple conviviality. The contrasting colours and shades portray a bright and hopeful future; but what we know with hindsight is that before 1945, some of them, even before the completion of their undergraduate careers, would be dead.

Remembrance Sunday is an important way of stirring our *collective* creative imagination. We have done this already by responding in silence to the reading of the names recorded on the Cloister walls; all those names, faceless but so vividly present, would also have once been known in this chapel before they left – for good. There is one other way that together we can reflect further on this theme of 'remembrance' – and that is more visually, through the chapel's iconography, particularly through one chapel window which stands out from the rest.

When William Burges designed this chapel in the 1860s, and when Henry Holiday executed his designs for the windows and the wall friezes, together they undoubtedly intended the nave –the body of the chapel, where you are- to be a colourful and even riotous celebration of life (so much so that some of the Fellows complained bitterly to Provost Cotton that such excessive and sensuous symbolism, which would lead to idolatry, should be removed). Even a quick glance at the wall panels, marked here and there with hints of humour, shows just how much attention was given to the fecundity of the natural world – as the green things, the fowls of the air, the children of men, the beasts and cattle, the seas and floods, the mountains and hills all become part of a paean of praise to the Creator God.

But the impression is very different when one is in the chancel. The most obvious contrast is the East Window, where, in a typically Pre-Raphaelite way, Holiday depicted Christ's suffering and death. Its subject matter, if not its style, marks it off from the rest of the chapel. Here we see the darkened sun and the crescent moon – even though the time of the dying is only midday. Instead of the celebration of Creation, this is humanity at its most vulnerable, most raw. We see the skull, the nails, the crown of thorns, the cross outside the city walls where only criminals died, and we sense the dereliction of Christ, deserted by all except his mother and closest disciple.

But the window is only one aspect of this dark contrast between chancel and nave. If you look below the window you will see the frieze directly behind the altar, above the dado, with Holiday's painting of Christ's entombment. It again is entirely different from the other friezes under the other windows. As in the window, we see Mary, mother of Jesus, and John, preparing Jesus' body for burial before the Sabbath begins, along with Mary Magdalene and Nicodemus. The frieze of the entombment takes us, chronologically, one stage further into the despair of the disciples because of the suffering and death of Christ.

There is another commentary on this window, much higher up, in a lunette close to the ceiling. You should be able to see an unfurled scroll with a few words just visible: it is typical of the other six lunettes above the other six windows. This one, however, has a text which is very different from the others, which speak of life and hope. This scroll speaks of suffering and death. It reads '[The] Messiah shall be cut off and shall have nothing'. These are words from the book of Daniel, which was our Old Testament reading. This passage in Daniel is full of complicated symbolism: it is in fact a code for a people in persecution. It is a review of some tragic events in their

The frieze of the Entombment.

The scroll of the prophet Daniel.

history, and the author is trying to assure them that these hard times will soon be over. He uses a numerical symbol, whereby a week consists not of seven days, but of seven years, in order to teach in code that although the people have been under foreign rule some 490 years, this will soon come to an end. Things will get worse before they get better – first an 'anointed one' (a priestly figure) will be 'cut off' and killed, then the sanctuary will be destroyed, and for some seven years anarchy will reign. Then everything will be reversed. The writer, posing as a legendary hero called Daniel, is actually referring to specific events in the second century BCE; the murdered anointed priest is probably Onias III, and the person destroying the sanctuary is probably Antiochus Epiphanes, a Greek Seleucid ruler.

I am quite sure that when Burges chose this text for the scroll he was not in the least bit interested in all this Maccabean history. What he wanted to offer in this prominent position was a text from *Daniel*; the name would call to mind both Wilson Eustace Daniel, who was Chaplain in 1864, the year of the formal reopening of the chapel, and his brother, Charles Henry Olive Daniel, Fellow and later Provost, who had both been so supportive of Burges' chapel designs. 'Daniel typology' was an important contemporary comment, and almost anything in the book of Daniel would have worked; but a text speaking about one who was 'anointed' and 'cut off' which illustrated so well the theme of the Crucifixion Window, was ideal. Furthermore, it was one of the few Old Testament texts which referred explicitly to an anointed one (or Messiah, the same name for Christ) who suffers and dies so that others may go free. So, with its Daniel wordplay, it was a most appropriate text in demonstrating that the suffering of Christ had been foretold in the Old Testament, and showing that the dreadful process of his dying was nevertheless a strange part of God's plan.

So this East Window shows us the Messiah, 'cut off' from the city and his people, being crucified on skull hill, the place where common criminals were killed. The skull under the cross is a vivid symbol of it all. As in Daniel, there is the echo of the 'destruction of the sanctuary'. This is picked up both literally, in that the curtain in the inner part of the Temple is described as being torn apart, and metaphorically, in that Jesus himself, a priestly figure, the 'sanctuary' of God's presence on Earth, is also being torn apart. Furthermore, above the cross is the title INRI, in Latin reading 'Jesus of Nazareth, King of the Jews'. Jesus had made it clear he was not an earthly king: his kingship, he had said to Pilate, was not of this world. This takes us back to the book of Daniel, which speaks of God's heavenly kingship over powers and dominions, and gives us a foretaste of the eventual victory of Christ over sin and death. But this is just a mere hint in this window. The real focus is on utter despair at the sight of the suffering, dying Christ.

There are a few places in the nave itself where the dying Christ is commemorated, but you can only see them properly if you stand on the chancel steps. These are on the dark walnut inlays on the pew-ends: one depicts three nails, another, a ladder to take Christ down from the cross, another, a crown of thorns, another, a spear, another, a seamless robe. The transformation from light and colour and humour to the bleaker and darker tones of death and distress in the chancel and on the wooden pew-ends is a striking part of the chapel's design; Burges certainly intended to make us take note – to 'remember' the crucifixion scene not only above us but around us.

There is an uncanny correlation between the sacrifice of Christ and the sacrifice of those who have died in war. They, too, are commemorated in those interminable war cemeteries, in Flanders fields and other battlefields of the world wars, by the symbol of the cross. The cross is of course a most powerful symbol: its vertical stake reaches down to the death and hell and up to new life in heaven, and its horizontal bar reaches out to embrace all of humanity, given new life by their death. The uncanny correlation goes beyond this. The war-torn dead, like the death of Christ, remind us that in the midst of life there is always sacrifice and death. They too can move us to profound gratitude and compassion, for in their act of self-giving we realise that what they achieved in death was the creation of new life for us. Their gift is, of course, material and temporal; the gift of Christ from the cross is also spiritual and eternal, because his death is only the first act of a story which encompasses new resurrection life as well. Nevertheless, taken together, their dying has given us the freedom which we enjoy daily and puts before us a debt we can never repay.

Innocent suffering and gruesome death leads to an inevitable question, which neither those with faith nor those without can ever really answer: 'If there is a God, how can he allow such dreadful suffering?' This East Window depicting the sufferings of Christ offers no quick, glib answer; but it can offer us hope. God in Christ *embraced* dreadful suffering; he is not detached from it. So this must also mean that God, in Christ, also *embraces* the sufferings of the war dead, whether recognised by them or not. 'Greater love hath no man than this, that a man lay down his life for his friends.'

'At the going down of the sun and in the morning we will remember them.' Our part in all this is profoundly simple. Alone and together, we *must* remember them: we must not forget the cost of their sacrifice – neither theirs, nor that of Jesus Christ – and, with our creative imagination, we must find our appropriate response. To return to the words of John McCrae:

To you from failing hands we throw
the torch; be yours to hold it high.
If ye break with us who die
We shall not sleep, though poppies grow
In Flanders fields…

From *In Flanders Fields and Other Poems* (1918)

Appendix
Daniel 9:24–27

[24] "Seventy weeks are decreed for your people and your holy city: to finish the transgression, to put an end to sin, and to atone for iniquity, to bring in everlasting righteousness, to seal both vision and prophet, and to anoint a most holy place. [25] Know therefore and understand: from the time that the word went out to restore and rebuild Jerusalem until the time of an anointed prince, there shall be seven weeks; and for sixty-two weeks it shall be built again with streets and moat, but in a troubled time. [26] After the sixty-two weeks, an anointed one shall be cut off and shall have nothing, and the troops of the prince who is to come shall destroy the city and the sanctuary. Its end shall come with a flood, and to the end there shall be war. Desolations are decreed. [27] He shall make a strong covenant with many for one week, and for half of the week he shall make sacrifice and offering cease; and in their place shall be an abomination that desolates, until the decreed end is poured out upon the desolator."

John 19:16–30

[16] Then he handed him over to them to be crucified. So they took Jesus; [17] and carrying the cross by himself, he went out to what is called The Place of the Skull, which in Hebrew is called Golgotha. [18] There they crucified him, and with him two others, one on either side, with Jesus between them. [19] Pilate also had an inscription written and put on the cross. It read, "Jesus of Nazareth, the King of the Jews." [20] Many of the Jews read this inscription, because the place where Jesus was crucified was near the city; and it was written in Hebrew, in Latin, and in Greek. [21] Then the chief priests of the Jews said to Pilate, "Do not write, 'The King of the Jews,' but, 'This man said, I am King of the Jews.'" [22] Pilate answered, "What I have written I have written." [23] When the soldiers had crucified Jesus, they took his clothes and divided them into four parts, one for each soldier. They also took his tunic; now the tunic was seamless, woven in one piece from the top. [24] So they said to one another, "Let us not tear it, but cast lots for it to see who will get it." This was to fulfill what the scripture says, "They divided my clothes among themselves, and for my clothing they cast lots." [25] And that is what the soldiers did. Meanwhile, standing near the cross of Jesus were his mother, and his mother's sister, Mary the wife of Clopas, and Mary Magdalene. [26] When Jesus saw his mother and the disciple whom he loved standing beside her, he said to his mother, "Woman, here is your son." [27] Then he said to the disciple, "Here is your mother." And from that hour the disciple took her into his own home. [28] After this, when Jesus knew that all was now finished, he said (in order to fulfill the scripture), "I am thirsty." [29] A jar full of sour wine was standing there. So they put a sponge full of the wine on a branch of hyssop and held it to his mouth. [30] When Jesus had received the wine, he said, "It is finished." Then he bowed his head and gave up his spirit.

The Resurrection Window

9 February 2004
Readings: Hosea 6:1–3; John 20:1–17

This sermon, on Mary Magdalene and the empty tomb, was part of a series on Encounters with Jesus in the Gospel of John

The Resurrection Window – the third window on the north side of the Chapel – is a skilful artistic comment on an event which, according to all four Gospels, is both in this world and not of it. The other-worldly dimension is clearly represented by the angelic figure in the heart of the stained glass. If one stands back a little, the similarities between this window and that of the Annunciation, the window also on the north side but nearest the door, are seen by the dominance of the angel – the rose-tinted wings (symbolising the purifying power of the Spirit) the white robes, the golden hair, the figure silhouetted by the deep blue sky and the vine leaves, symbols of fecundity and new life – and the figure of a woman below with a halo signifying her saintliness, looking upwards.

There are differences, of course: the woman in the Annunciation is Mary, mother-to-be of Jesus, and the woman in the Resurrection scene is Mary Magdalene, one of Jesus' closest followers. But the two scenes: of miraculous beginnings, mediated by an angel, and of miraculous endings, mediated by another angel – are deliberately brought together. Both are scenes in which visual exegesis – communicating the mysterious, the paradoxical, the other-worldly – perhaps works better in this genre than in more limited narrative account.

The Resurrection Window develops the ethereal dimension still further: if you look at the gilt frieze under it, you will see a group of angelic beings (this is the only such frieze in the chapel, the

The angelic figures in the Resurrection and Annunciation windows.

The frieze of angelic beings (under the Resurrection Window).

five others like it being of human beings – saints, prophets, martyrs, apostles, and ordinary human folk). There is Uriel, Raphael (with his fish), Gabriel (with the lily, as in the Annunciation Window), Michael (with his sword, perhaps the same figure as in the Resurrection Window above), and a choir of eight angels, all singing praises to God.

But this is not some apocalyptic vision of angelic beings. The scene is also, paradoxically, rooted in human history. The first indication of its historical setting is the prophetic scroll above the window. This is a fragment of a text taken from the prophet Hosea: 'After two days will he revive us: in the third day he will raise us up.' This illustrates that the miraculous event of the empty tomb, mediated here through the angel, was in fact prophesied some eight hundred years previously: in short, it is all part of some preordained divine plan from God for human history. (The prophet Hosea is actually referring to an event in his own day, speaking in metaphorical terms of the return of the people of Israel to their own land; but from a Christian perspective, it describes so precisely the death and restoration – after three days – of Jesus Christ. So the use of this text is a way of claiming a divine origin for the mystery of the empty tomb.)

If the scroll above the window affirms that the resurrection scene is neither entirely strange nor inexplicable, but rather an expected part of human history, there are two other ways in which Burges' designs bring this event directly into our history.

The scroll of the prophet Hosea.

The most obvious is the depiction of the human figures in the window itself: the woman with the long blonde hair (perhaps more Pre-Raphaelite than a more dark-haired Middle Eastern woman) who is looking up at the angel is Mary Magdalene. The other two figures represent other women who came with Mary early in the morning, bringing spices to leave at what they had assumed would be an enclosed tomb. Their terror and bewilderment at seeing the stone rolled away from the rock-cut tomb

(this can be seen on the far left of the window) and the figure in white robes, with burnished wings, are captured in the face of the older woman, who is looking away in fear and disbelief, and in the anonymous figure (probably also a woman) shielding and comforting Mary Magdalene.

Another way the this-worldly focus in this extraordinary scene is achieved is in the wall panels on either side of the window. These are also unusual: they are small white cameos, and each depicts different characters – rich and poor, leaders and layfolk, craftsmen and mothers; there is a bishop, a king, a doctor and a lawyer, yet also a poet, a nun, a carpenter, a mother and a fisherman. The event in the window, with all its terrifying other-worldly dimensions, witnessing to the one who had faced death yet defied it, is nevertheless rooted in human history. Some of its interpreters are more divine than human; but others are certainly more human than divine.

One of the real problems in looking at the details of this window is determining which account in which Gospel Burges was in fact using. The four accounts of the discovery of the empty tomb are all very different in their details: Luke has two angels, and refers to Mary Magdalene, Joanna, Mary, the mother of James, 'and other women' coming to the tomb. So given that there is one angel, and only three women, the account is unlikely to be from Luke. Matthew narrates an earthquake, and speaks of 'guards' standing by the tomb, and two women who are both called Mary, and just one angel. So again, Burges' source is unlikely to be Matthew. Mark speaks of three women at the tomb, as well as a 'man in white': but Mark's account also emphasises not only that the women were terrified, but also that they fled and told no one of what they had seen. The actual details on this window – the three women and the man in white – fit more closely with Mark, but the element of celebration in this window – underscored by the angels praising God in the scene below – hardly fits with the more negative tenor of the terror of the women in Mark. John describes succinctly and clearly that the stone rolled away, but he speaks of two angels, and he makes it clear that Mary Magdalene on her own witnessed not only this event but also encountered Jesus himself in the garden; so again, it is difficult to see how this account matches with what we see in the window.

Taking the interesting comparison between the Annunciation Window and this Resurrection Window, I cannot help opting for an interpretation which is based on John's Gospel but one which also uses some of the details of Mark. In the Annunciation Window, the only figure encountering the angel is Mary of Nazareth; and in the Resurrection Window, the key figure encountering the angel is another woman, Mary of Magdalene. What we could be seeing in this window, then, is an event which follows the one we heard read from John's Gospel earlier tonight. In John's account, Mary is quite clearly alone; but because in that account she has the courage to look inside the tomb, this may then have been her second visit there, leaving her friends behind, and returning to see exactly what had taken place. Admittedly there is still a problem because John tells us that she saw *two* figures dressed in white, but, more importantly, she also sees the tomb is completely empty. John implies that Mary can only presume that the body – linen cloths and all – has been *stolen*. He tells us how she hears a voice: 'Woman, why are you weeping?' and she replies 'Because they've taken my Lord, and I don't know where they've laid him'. Sensing a figure outside the face of the tomb, she turns around. The figure asks her the same question – hasn't he heard what she had just said? – 'Woman, why are you weeping? *Whom do you seek?*' At this early hour, with so many distracting thoughts, she can only suppose he is the gardener. 'Sir, if you've taken him, tell me where he is. I will

take him away and give him the burial he deserves.' This figure speaks just one word: 'Mary'. In this recognition of her name, two worlds collide: the world of death, her loss and obvious bereavement, and the promise of a life beyond, a journey into the unknown. She hears, and she believes, although she certainly does not understand. 'Rabboni!' is all she says. Seeking assurance, she comes forward and attempts to embrace her risen Lord, but he prevents her; this is not the time for physical certainties. 'Go, tell my disciples that I am ascending to my Father and your Father, to my God and your God'. John concludes his Gospel story as tersely as he began it, underplaying the trauma of it all: 'Mary went and said to the disciples, "I have seen the Lord"'.

The two 'Mother and Child' cameos on each side of the window.

The beginning of the Gospel is about the crucial role of a woman, and at the end God similarly entrusts the Good News to a woman. Mary Magdalene was the first to see the risen Christ (although, admittedly, in this window all she and her companions saw was an angel, but as I have argued, what John is telling is the later and final act of the story), and Mary Magdalene is entrusted as the first witness who must now share it with others; this has so many parallels with Mary of Nazareth, who brought the Christ-Child into the world, and who was the first to share the enormity of this burden with others. Many taboos were shattered, not only at the beginning of the Gospel story but also at the end of it: a woman was entrusted with the bearing of the life of the Son of God, and a woman was entrusted with testifying to the two most important aspects of Jesus' resurrection – his empty tomb, and his appearing again.

Mary Magdalene, from Magdala in Galilee, is undoubtedly the heroine in this Resurrection Window. She was the one whom (we know from Luke's account) supported Jesus in his earthly ministry from her private means; she was the one whom we also know from Luke was healed by Jesus of some demon possession; she was the one who washed Jesus' feet with her hair and horrified those present at such gestures of intimacy. This Mary, reformed prostitute and close companion of Jesus, was the first and primary witness to his resurrection. Traditional norms and expectations – the traditional Jewish view of all women bearing the mark of the disobedience of Eve in another Garden – were turned upside down by the response of another woman in another garden – the garden which, in its midst, held Christ's tomb.

It is difficult to know if, through these two corresponding windows of the Annunciation and the Resurrection, Burges intended to make any theological or political comment on the place of women for his own day. It was not till some fifteen years after the chapel was refurbished, in 1879, that women were allowed in some small measure into the male bastion of Oxford learning, although, even then, they could only attend lectures with special permission, and could not take the same honours examinations as men. And if women's role in society was constrained, their role in the church was even more so. So to credit Burges with such a radical vision may be going further than he intended. However, as far as the church and its role in society today are concerned, the theological and social challenge behind these two windows could not be more pertinent. Over the last century and a half we have become so aware of the prejudice, confusion, perplexity and resistance to change when it comes to female authority in the church. In countering these firmly held beliefs, Mary's cry 'Rabboni', and Jesus's response 'Go, tell my disciples that I am ascending to my Father and your Father' echo across the centuries. Mary's 'Rabboni: my Teacher!' is the cry of all women seeking to serve their church, and Jesus' 'Go to the brethren and say to them… "I have seen the Lord"' is one that cannot be ignored. This window testifies in part to the first apostolic witness which began with Mary at the Garden Tomb, and it still serves as a challenge to the church today.

Appendix
Hosea 6:1–3
[1] "Come, let us return to the LORD; for it is he who has torn, and he will heal us; he has struck down, and he will bind us up. [2] After two days he will revive us; on the third day he will raise us up, that we may live before him. [3] Let us know, let us press on to know the LORD; his appearing is as sure as the dawn; he will come to us like the showers, like the spring rains that water the earth."

John 20:1–17
[1] Early on the first day of the week, while it was still dark, Mary Magdalene came to the tomb and saw that the stone had been removed from the tomb. [2] So she ran and went to Simon Peter and the other disciple, the one whom Jesus loved, and said to them, "They have taken the Lord out of the tomb, and we do not know where they have laid him." [3] Then Peter and the other disciple set out and went toward the tomb. [4] The two were running together, but the other disciple outran Peter and reached the tomb first. [5] He bent down to look in and saw the linen wrappings lying there, but he did not go in. [6] Then Simon Peter came, following him, and went into the tomb. He saw the linen wrappings lying there, [7] and the cloth that had been on Jesus' head, not lying with the linen wrappings but rolled up in a place by itself. [8] Then the other disciple, who reached the tomb first, also went in, and he saw and believed; [9] for as yet they did not understand the scripture, that he must rise from the dead. [10] Then the disciples returned to their homes. [11] But Mary stood weeping outside the tomb. As she wept, she bent over to look into the tomb; [12] and she saw two angels in white, sitting where the body of Jesus had been lying, one at the head and the other at the feet. [13] They said to her, "Woman, why are you weeping?" She said to them, "They have taken away my Lord, and I do not know where they have laid him." [14] When she had said this, she turned around and saw Jesus standing there, but she did not know that it was Jesus. [15] Jesus said to her, "Woman, why are you weeping? Whom are you looking for?" Supposing him to be the gardener, she said to him, "Sir, if you have carried him away, tell me where you have laid him, and I will take him away." [16] Jesus said to her, "Mary!" She turned and said to him in Hebrew, "Rabboni!" (which means Teacher). [17] Jesus said to her, "Do not hold on to me, because I have not yet ascended to the Father. But go to my brothers and say to them, 'I am ascending to my Father and your Father, to my God and your God.'"

The Ascension Window

6 March 2005
Readings: Psalm 68: 7–20; Luke 24:44–53

This sermon was the last in a series on the Lord's Prayer, looking at the final phrase 'For Thine is the Kingdom, the Power and the Glory, for ever and for ever'

One of the most interesting things about the final doxology of the Lord's Prayer, the subject of this sermon series tonight, is that some versions leave it in, and others entirely forget it. We have prayed the Lord's Prayer twice in this service, but we only used this doxology the first time, when, as a congregation, we said it together. When the choir sang the Lord's Prayer for us the second time, the doxology was left out. In almost all the recent translations of the Bible into English, it doesn't occur at all – whether in the longer version of Matthew (6:9–13) or in the crisper version of Luke (11:2–4), the Lord's Prayer ends with *'Deliver us from evil'*.

So you might well ask whether it is worth preaching on this final ending at all: it isn't found in any of the earliest Greek manuscripts and the Latin-speaking churches of the West almost never used it. Its first occurrence is in a catechetical document used by the Eastern churches in Syria, called the Didache, dating from the second century. Its first appearance in English is in Tyndale's 1534 translation of the New Testament (and this might perhaps be because Tyndale preferred the traditions of the Eastern churches to those of what he saw as the 'more corrupt' Catholic West). The translators of the King James Version, or what we now call the Authorised Version, dating from 1611, followed Tyndale; this is why if you looked in the Authorised Version, which we use in chapel, you would find it, even though it is one of the very few English versions to have it. And because the Authorised Version influenced the 1662 Prayer Book, which is the form of service we have been using tonight, it was included here, too – but only once, at the beginning of the service. At other times it is omitted.

So given that it's used in some versions and not in others, what difference might its addition make to the prayer as a whole? If we take the shortened version, the Lord's Prayer falls neatly into two parts, starting with a recognition of who God is, and ending an admission of our need for Him. So the first half has three acclamations praising God for who he is – His Name (*'hallowed be Thy Name'*) His Kingdom (*'Thy Kingdom come'*) His Will (*'Thy Will be done'*); the second half has three petitions appealing to God to meet our needs – our physical needs (*'give us this day our daily bread'*), our spiritual needs (*'forgive us our trespasses'*), and our temptations and trials (*'lead us not into temptation but deliver us from evil'*). However, if we take the longer version, we have a prayer which starts and ends with a threefold acclamation of who God is – His Name, His Kingdom, His Will at the beginning, His Kingdom, His Power, and His Glory at the end. So only the middle section is about our needs, which, in the light of who God is, takes on a different, more minimalist emphasis.

However, in spite of the fact that the earliest Greek versions in Matthew and Luke both use the shorter version, the phrase *'For yours is the kingdom, the power and the glory'* was known in a different context in Jesus' day. It occurs frequently in the Old Testament; for example, it comes in Solomon's prayer at the dedication of the Temple in 1 Chronicles (29:11) – a prayer which we sometimes use today when the collection is brought up to the altar: *'Thine, O Lord, is the greatness, and the Power,*

The scroll of the 'prophet' David.

and the Glory ... and the Kingdom ... for all that is in the heaven and in the earth is thine...'. It comes several times in the Psalms. Psalm 145:11–12 praises God in this way: *'All your works shall speak of the Glory of your Kingdom, and tell of your Power...'.*

Many Christians rarely realise that every single phrase of the doxology of the Lord's Prayer has its roots in the Old Testament; this should not be surprising, however, as Christian prayer was closely related to its Jewish origins. Take, for example, the initial address to God as 'Our Father', the expression about God dwelling in heaven, the acclamation of God's holy name, and the petitions for bread, for forgiveness, and for protection in temptation: the Lord's Prayer is full of easily memorable phrases from its rich Old Testament heritage. The uniqueness of the Lord's Prayer is not in the ideas *per se*, but in the ways in which Jesus interwove them into a single prayer to God.

So this doxology, even though it might have been a late addition to our Western worship, is nevertheless rooted in ancient, Jewish thinking about God. So the most important question we are left with is – what does it *mean* to speak of God's Kingdom and Power and Glory in this way?

The Old Testament is very graphic about the way it depicts God 'ruling' both in heaven and on Earth. One way of doing so was through ritual enactment of the reign of God in worship. For example, in earliest times, the Ark – a sort of chest containing the laws which had a throne placed upon it – was processed up to the Temple, and the moment of its arrival symbolised God's earthly and heavenly thrones converging together. Examples of this liturgy are found in the Psalms. Psalm 24, for example, speaks of the Ark entering Jerusalem as if God, too, is going in to the city: *'Lift up your heads, O gates! And be lifted up, O ancient doors! that the King of Glory may come in. Who is the King of Glory? The Lord of hosts, he is the King of Glory!'.* Another very ancient psalm, which also focuses on God's Kingdom, God's Power, and God's Glory is Psalm 68 (vv. 24 and 18): *'Thy solemn processions are seen, O God, into the sanctuary … Thou hast ascended on high, thou hast led captivity captive…'.*

We heard part of Psalm 68 in our Old Testament reading earlier tonight. It was a deliberate choice. For here in this chapel, we have a vivid visual reminder of what it means to acclaim, as Christians, that the Kingdom, the Power and the Glory are God's alone. The words are found on the scroll in the lunette above the window which depicts Christ's Ascension. Each of the seven windows, designed by William Burges, has a scroll above it. The other six windows use verses from the prophets; this window, reading David the psalmist as 'a prophet', records the words of Psalm 68 – you might just be able to read the words *'Thou hast ascended on high'.* They have been chosen to show that yet again verses from the Old Testament are like prophecies fulfilled in the life and death of Jesus: this one is being fulfilled in Christ's own 'ascending on high'.

If you look at the window underneath this scroll, you will see how Burges designed the scene of Christ's 'Ascending' so that it simultaneously retained a this-worldly and an other-worldly dimension. The this-worldly dimension is clear, and its depiction of Christ's Ascension here could not be more different from other representations of it, usually behind the high altar. I think of the vast mosaic depicting Christ in Glory behind the high altar in Keble Chapel, and the overpowering figure of Christ in Glory behind the high altar of St Barnabas' Church, Jericho, for example. The scene is not even set within the East Window: Burges preferred the crucifixion scene to dominate this liturgical space, and so contained the Ascension scene within the south side of the chapel. But even so, the window here is strikingly different from another medieval version in stained glass on the south side of a church: I am thinking here of John Keble's parish church, St Mary's, Fairford, where in that window all one sees of Christ's Ascension 'up' to heaven is his feet, surrounded by clouds. Our window is undoubtedly more earthly: all of Christ is visible here, with his hands raised in a priestly blessing. He is not presented as an angel (you can see the way that angels were depicted in the window directly opposite, for example) but as one who has not quite yet physically left this world. He is still very much in some relationship with his disciples: there are echoes here of the Transfiguration scene on that mountain in Galilee, before Peter, James and John. Nevertheless, there is a difference. The other-worldly dimension is evident not only in the whiteness of his robes and the clear iconic outline, but also in his eyes, which tell us that the risen Christ has another world in view. The flaming red trees behind this outline also testify to it: every window in this chapel has some form of symbolic foliage, and here this is used to give hints of that terrifying revelation made to Moses through the Burning Bush. Here too is the evocation of fire, and with this, of strength and power. So this encounter between Christ and his six disciples is still in this world, whilst also testifying to a world beyond it: we see here not only the incarnate authority of Christ, but also the coming fire of the Spirit. And, between these times, we can also intuit a sense of real urgency: for the ongoing extension of his work on Earth, Christ depends upon the how these six will respond to him from this time on.

When we consider this window in relation to other windows of the chapel, we see how cleverly Burges has constructed this theme of Jesus, the one who both brings the Kingdom of God to Earth and the one who allows those of us on Earth a vision of the Kingdom of God in heaven. The first window

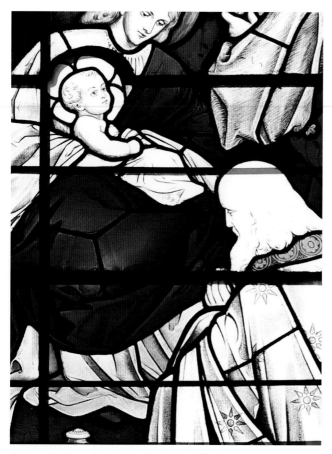 

The worship of one of the kings in the Epiphany Window.　　　　　*The worship of three disciples in the Ascension Window.*

on this south wall, nearest the Provost's Stall, has an identical theme. This is of the visit of the three kings to Bethlehem, just after Jesus' birth: like the six disciples in our Ascension Window, the kings in this Epiphany window are poised in different states of adoration, bewilderment and awe: their gaze may be on the baby Jesus rather than the ascending Christ, but the sense that this is about the breaking in of the kingdom of God into this world is the same: 'We have come to see him who has been born King of the Jews'. The scroll above this window has the same theme: from Zechariah 14:9, it reads, 'And the Lord will become king over all the earth'. These two windows, therefore, echo one another. God's Kingdom, God's Power and God's Glory is first disguised through the innocence of the infant Jesus, and finally revealed though the figure of the ascended Christ. If you look closely at the faces of the kings, their different responses are echoed in the different responses on the faces of the disciples as they gaze on the dazzling white robes of Christ: fear, bemusement, relief, disbelief, awe, and attempt at faith.

Given that this window captures the scene of the Ascension, it is important to note in finishing how peculiar this scene is. Neither Matthew's Gospel nor John's Gospel records it at all; and even in Mark, it comes in one verse in an ending to the Gospel which has been left out of many manuscripts. So it is only Luke who includes it in full – and even he seems uncertain as to when it took place, because when he records it at the end of the Gospel he sets the story in Easter week, but at the beginning of Acts he has set it some forty days later. So if those closest to the event had some trouble understanding what happened, we might be excused by also being confused about its place in history. It seems to me that it is more important to imagine the scene – to try to understand it symbolically and theologically – rather than try to track down the precise details of what really happened. And so we are brought again to the significance of this window, where in our imagination we can enter into the event, and find ourselves merging with the disciples – like them, fearful and not understanding, terrified but trying to believe.

One of the most reassuring aspects of this window is the frieze beneath it. The other friezes are of saints, martyrs, prophets, apostles, and even an angelic host. This one is, very simply, of ordinary layfolk. They are the ones who have received the message of the Kingdom of God, in this world but not of it, from those who were closest to Christ, and they are the ones who will pass this message on. You can see three women here – a nun, a sister of mercy, a mother. You can see an artist, a carpenter, a farmer, a fisherman. They intermingle with a bishop, king, knight, poet and lawyer: and in all probability Burges has given each of them, whatever their station in life, personae of people he knew. But these in their different ways are responding to the iconic figure in white above them – the one who revealed the Kingdom, Power and Glory of God in a human life, who now blesses us, yet at the same time points us beyond earthly perceptions to heavenly realities. These are the ones who, like us, viewing the same scene as them, have to determine how to respond to the convergence of two worlds – that of God's earthly dwelling with them, and that of God's utter otherness from them.

They, along with the six disciples above, are given the same challenge, and it is one which also is given to us. Will we come to recognise that Jesus Christ is the prism through whom God's Kingdom is most clearly seen, in all its vulnerability from birth to death, and in all its Power and Glory in this life into the life beyond?

'Thou hast ascended on high.'
'Thine is the Kingdom, the Power and the Glory.'

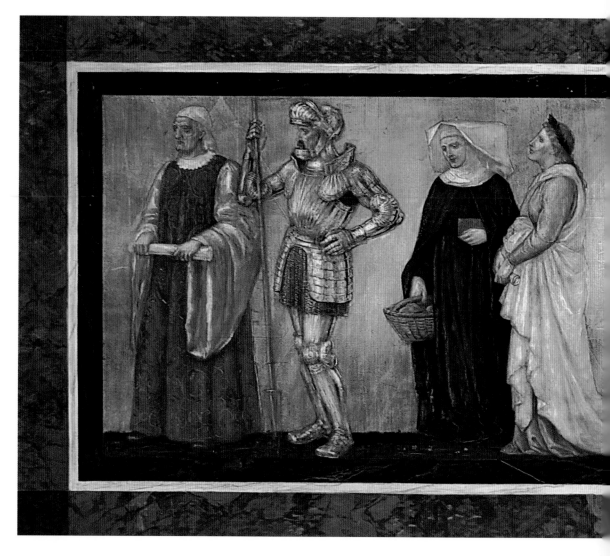

Appendix

Psalm 68:7–20

[7] O God, when you went out before your people, when you marched through the wilderness, Selah [8] the earth quaked, the heavens poured down rain at the presence of God, the God of Sinai, at the presence of God, the God of Israel. [9] Rain in abundance, O God, you showered abroad; you restored your heritage when it languished; [10] your flock found a dwelling in it; in your goodness, O God, you provided for the needy. [11] The Lord gives the command; great is the company of those who bore the tidings: [12] 'The kings of the armies, they flee, they flee!' The women at home divide the spoil, [13] though they stay among the sheepfolds – the wings of a dove covered with silver, its pinions with green gold. [14] When the Almighty scattered kings there, snow fell on Zalmon. [15] O mighty mountain, mountain of Bashan; O many-peaked mountain, mountain of Bashan! [16] Why do you look with envy, O many-peaked mountain, at the mount that God desired for his abode, where the LORD will reside forever? [17] With mighty chariotry, twice ten thousand, thousands upon thousands, the Lord came from Sinai into the holy place. [18] You ascended the high mount, leading captives in your train and receiving gifts from people, even from those who rebel against the LORD

God's abiding there. [19] Blessed be the Lord, who daily bears us up; God is our salvation. Selah [20] Our God is a God of salvation, and to GOD, the Lord, belongs escape from death.

Luke 24:44–53

[44] Then he said to them, 'These are my words that I spoke to you while I was still with you – that everything written about me in the law of Moses, the prophets, and the psalms must be fulfilled.' [45] Then he opened their minds to understand the scriptures, [46] and he said to them, 'Thus it is written, that the Messiah is to suffer and to rise from the dead on the third day, [47] and that repentance and forgiveness of sins is to be proclaimed in his name to all nations, beginning from Jerusalem. [48] You are witnesses of these things. [49] And see, I am sending upon you what my Father promised; so stay here in the city until you have been clothed with power from on high.' [50] Then he led them out as far as Bethany, and, lifting up his hands, he blessed them. [51] While he was blessing them, he withdrew from them and was carried up into heaven. [52] And they worshipped him, and returned to Jerusalem with great joy; [53] and they were continually in the temple blessing God.

The Te Deum

4 March 2007
Readings: Daniel 7: 9–14; Revelation 4:1–11

The Canticle was sung by the Choir as an Anthem (to Orlando Gibbons' 'Short Service')

The sermon was the last of a series of nine on the iconography of the chapel, and also the last in a term's series on the Beatitudes: 'Blessed are those who are persecuted for righteousness' sake, for theirs is the Kingdom of God'.

The first sermon on the iconography of the chapel was in 2001, just after its restoration was completed. That was on the Benedicite, a morning canticle whose text is set high up above the cornice with the illustrations of it mainly on the walls and pew carvings. Since then I have given seven other sermons, all on the chapel windows. This, the final sermon, focuses on the Te Deum, which is another traditional morning canticle, like the Benedicite. In the case of the Te Deum, the text is set below the windows and below the dado, somewhat surprisingly discreetly hidden. Whereas Burges chose to give the Benedicite full exposure, he buried the Te Deum behind the backs of the pews. Having heard it sung so magnificently by our choir as the anthem just before this sermon, you may well wonder why.

But first, you might well ask, why did Burges choose these two canticles at all? They are best known as morning hymns and are rarely sung at Matins, let alone Evensong, these days. The answer is quite simple. When the chapel was refurbished in the 1860s, attendance was compulsory, and the time when most college members worshipped was the morning. Since then most of the sung college services have gradually moved to the evening. So Burges was in fact using texts which would be most familiar to that nineteenth-century congregation – part of a liturgical discourse we can no longer recognise.

The Benedicite is a repeated call *to all the natural order* to praise God: 'O all ye Green Things upon the Earth… O all ye Fowls of the Air… O all ye Beasts and Cattle… O all ye Seas and Floods… bless ye the Lord…'. Each of these calls to worship, set high in the chapel, is illustrated on the walls below each call, in the panels on each side of a stained-glass window. For example, you can see foliage and fruits represented on the panels under the call to the 'Green Things' to praise God, and you can see the fishes (both small and great) on the panels below the call to the 'Seas and Floods'; and on the panels calling upon the 'Beasts and Cattle' to bless the Lord', various wild animals have been depicted, as also in the carvings on the pews. This is done with a touch of

The dodo is called upon to fly and 'bless the Lord'.

*'Holy – Holy – Holy – **God** …'. The Provost's Stall. '*   *Wep – **raise** – Thee – O God …'. The Vice-Provost's Stall.*

humour: in the panel calling upon the 'Fowls of the Air' you can see several birds, both flying but also non-flying – and the dodo, for good measure, has also been carved on one of the pew-ends.

The Te Deum is very different. It is not so much a many-faceted call *upon creation* to bless God, as a hymn beginning with 'us', uniting *all humanity* with the heavenly host in praise of God: 'We praise thee O God, we acknowledge Thee to be the Lord … All the earth doth worship thee, the Father everlasting. To thee all Angels cry aloud, the Heavens, and all the Powers therein. To thee Cherubim and Seraphim continually do cry, Holy, Holy, Holy, Lord God of Sabaoth'. (The canticle continues at length, but these are the words Burges selected for the chapel.) But instead of the text being written high up in the chapel for all to see, it is written in gold inlay on the walnut backs of the pews, deep against the walls; and to make matters more esoteric and hidden, the words are deliberately scrambled. For example, the first line ('We praise thee O God, we acknowledge Thee to be the Lord…' runs from the Vice-Provost's Stall up to the end of the second window: 'wep – raise – thee – OGod – weac – kno – wle – dge – the – eto – beth – eLo – rda …'. And when we come to the last line ('and seraphim continually do cry, "Holy Holy Holy Lord, God of Hosts"') we read (starting at almost the same point but on the opposite side of the chapel and working otwards the back) 'nan – dse – rap – hin – conti – nua – lly – doc – ryh – oly – holy – holy – Lord – God – ofh – osts'. Whether this is intended to emulate some heavenly language or some secret code is unclear: but Burges' humour is very much part of this, for on the back of the Vice-Provost's Stall he has placed so clearly the word 'raise', and on the back of the Provost's Stall, we find, simply, the word 'God'.

The lines of the Te Deum not written out on the pews are picked up in six friezes just under each of the windows on the north and south walls (the East Window is different), and here we find six groups of saints, of martyrs, of prophets, of apostles, of angels and of ordinary layfolk – all of whom are called upon to join in the praise of God in later parts of the hymn. So just as the wall panels testify to the Benedicite, the friezes do likewise with the Te Deum. Furthermore, just as the Benedicite is represented more physically in the wooden animal carvings, the Te Deum is carved around the alabaster lectern in the middle of the chapel, a feature which when seen close up is as striking as the wooden animals on the pew-ends.

The first use of the Te Deum in Christian worship dates somewhere between the second and fourth centuries CE. Like the Benedicite, it is also found in Chapter Twelve of the 'Rule of Benedict',

A group of singers praising God on the alabaster lectern.

where it is called 'The Hymn of Ambrose' and is required to be sung at Matins every Sunday: the Benedictines who once worshipped on this site would thus have known this canticle well. Its origins lie in the time when the church was expanding yet persecuted, and its overall theme – rather like that of the Benedicite – is that the *praise of God can counter the fear of men*. However, unlike the Benedicite, it is not a hymn which is found in Scripture, but rather a later composition, usually connected with one of two fathers of the Western church – either Hilary of Poitiers or Ambrose of Milan (Ambrose is linked with the canticle by Benedict, and is immortalised by Burges in the mosaic floor of the chapel, nearest the chancel).

Even some one hundred and fifty years ago, the Te Deum would have been more familiar to those who worshipped in this chapel than it is today. It would have been sung more regularly at Matins, and the congregation then would have appreciated the humour of de-coding it – as a donnish joke in the manner of Lewis Carroll – on the backs of the pews. The music as well as the words would have been well known: it was frequently sung not only in imitations of Gregorian chant, but also in compositions by Mozart, Berlioz and Haydn. (Later the canticle was further 'popularised' – by Bruckner, Dvorak, Britten and Walton, who made an arrangement for the Queen's Coronation in 1952; the setting by Charpentier even made it into the Eurovision Song Contest, but most of us have probably forgotten all that by now.)

Just as the twelve verses from the Benedicite are selections of a much longer work, so too Burges selected only a small part of the Te Deum, taking verses from the first and oldest part of the hymn, which centres on praise to God the Father. (The second part of the Te Deum is of praise to Christ,

Uriel and Raphael.   *Gabriel and Michael.*

the suffering Son of God, and the third part, taken from various psalms, is about mercy and forgiveness; each of these is already illustrated in the rest of the chapel.) Whereas the words of the Benedicite are seven times accompanied by artistic representations in the panels below, the words of the Te Deum are illustrated in the friezes directly above, taking up the entire space just below six of the seven windows. In these friezes we see the angels, the prophets, the apostles, the martyrs, the saints and the Universal Church giving praises to God.

So first, on the north side, near the altar, we have the angels: 'to thee all Angels cry aloud'. Here we see Uriel and Raphael (with his fish), and Gabriel (with a lily) and Michael (with his sword) and their 'choir of eight', making music and singing 'Holy Holy, Holy, Lord God of Hosts'.

Then, on the middle frieze on the south side of the chapel, we have the apostles: 'The glorious company of the Apostles praise Thee'. Here we see all twelve apostles, including Peter with the Key to the gates of heaven and hell, and Andrew, with his cross.

The third illustration is of the prophets: 'The goodly fellowship of the Prophets praise Thee'. This frieze is directly opposite that of the apostles, next to that of the angels. The collection of prophets here complements the lunettes of the eight Old Testament prophets, each holding a scroll, seven above the seven windows and Ezekiel as the eighth under the entrance to the chapel. Isaiah and Daniel, who are represented in the lunettes, are for some reason repeated in this frieze. David and Solomon are also (somewhat idiosyncratically) represented as prophets, although on the dome of the chapel they are depicted as kings. Overall, the selection is quite surprising, and the presence of 'prophetesses' is even more so. There are ancient so-called prophets such as Enoch, Noah, Moses and Miriam – singing and dancing – and then David and Solomon, the latter of whom is holding a model of his Temple, and Huldah, Isaiah, Daniel, Malachi, and then, in a New Testament setting, John the Baptist and Anna.

Peter and his Key to heaven and hell.

Andrew and his cross.

The prophets Enoch and Noah.

The prophet Moses and the prophetess Miriam.

The Holy Innocents.

Cecilia, patron saint of Music.

The fourth illustration is of the martyrs of the church – 'The noble army of martyrs praise Thee'. These are found next to the prophets, nearest to the West Door, and form another rather diverse group which includes two angels protecting two children as the Holy Innocents killed by Herod, as well as Stephen, Polycarp, Thomas of Canterbury, Catherine (with her wheel), Perpetua, Cecilia (with her pipes), Jan Huss, Jerome of Prague, and Latimer and Hooper (both Bishops of Worcester).

The fifth illustration of 'the church throughout all the world' is found in two places. One is in the frieze of well-known saints and the other is the one of layfolk who come from all walks of life. The saints are behind the choir stalls on the north side: they comprise Augustine, Ambrose, Monica, Helena, King Olaf of Norway, sporting the ginger beard of Olive Daniel, the Fellow who unstintingly supported Burges' designs) along with Benedict (who might be called the founder of the college, as is evident in his depiction to the left of the entombment above the altar), as well as Catherine of Siena, Elizabeth of Hungary and Wycliffe – with his Bible – and Luther and Pascal.

Catherine of Siena and Elizabeth of Hungary.

The Universal Church – represented by lay men and women (especially the latter) of all ranks and none – is on the south side, nearest the altar. There are a bishop, a king, a doctor, a knight, a nun, a sister of mercy, a poet, a lawyer (with his red tape), an artist, a carpenter, a farmer, a mother, and a fisherman. To bring this message home, Burges took some artistic license by painting in this frieze some of the faces of people known in Oxford in his day.

So the Te Deum, in both words and pictures, moves from the praises of the heavenly host, above and beyond human time, to the praises of the apostles, prophets, martyrs and saints, within human time but beyond the hopes and aspirations of the congregation, to the praises of anyone and everyone, regardless of status or calling. By implication, this latter category includes those of us here in Chapel tonight: we too can join this distinguished host in its paean of praise. This is an appeal both to our intellect and to our imagination, as we are invited to become part of that great community of faith, throughout the entire world and throughout the entire history of the church, a company giving praise to God in every place at every time and in every circumstance.

Many – indeed, most – of the figures portrayed in the friezes are part of a suffering church; their praise is all the more sincere because it comes from persecution and hardship, which are ultimately overwhelmed by praise. This was the theme of our readings from Daniel and Revelation; each depicted how release from suffering comes when God's saints move from lamenting their own condition to becoming lost in the praise of God. In Daniel, this was what the faithful Jewish community in

Catherine, with her wheel.

Two Bishops of Worcester: Latimer and Hooper.

Jerusalem had to learn, persecuted because they refused to bow the knee to Antiochus Epiphanes, the then Greek ruler. In Revelation, this was what the faithful Christian community throughout Asia Minor had also to learn, because they refused to bow the knee to the might of Rome and worship its gods. We might well ask, what is the corresponding challenge, in Oxford, today?

This sermon is not only part of a series on the the chapel's iconography; it is also part of a sermon series on the Beatitudes which has been running throughout this term. You *might* ask how these readings and these reflections on the Te Deum have anything to do with the Beatitudes, not least our final one, 'Blessed are those who are persecuted for righteousness sake, for theirs is the Kingdom of God'. To this I would reply: a commentary on this Beatitude is not only expressed in our readings in Daniel and Revelation, but it is also to be found all around you. It is found in the apostles, prophets, martyrs, saints and indeed the whole church of God surround us, suffering communities and suffering individuals, persecuted for righteousness' sake, yet 'blessed' in their suffering because they have learned to transform their pain into an experience of God – Father, Son and Holy Ghost.

As for the Beatitudes, several preachers this term have commented on their 'upside-down' appeal. Stephen Cottrell, Bishop of Reading, observed how they 'offer a topsy-turvy view of life', which was not surprising in that they were spoken by Jesus, who turned the values of the world upside down and inside out. Tom Wright, Bishop of Durham, also reflected on the way that the Beatitudes reversed the world's values, and he said they were really about reality 'the right way up'. Certainly this final Beatitude, which affirms blessings for those who suffer innocently, belongs to this same topsy-turvy view of life.

'Blessed are those who are persecuted for righteousness' sake.' Innocent suffering is something we all have to face at one time or another. Sometimes it is physical; at others, mental or emotional; it can also be a profound spiritual pain, when we feel deprived of, yet yearn for, the presence of God. Innocent suffering is a real test as to how we live out our faith within a finite and often evil world. By far the most important comfort in our suffering is to realise that we are not alone. Suffering is the hallmark of the Christian faith, as is all too evident, for example, in the East Window, and it reminds us that the servants cannot expect less than their Master. So when it comes to pain and persecution, and indignation that this is undeserved, and our own ability to pray is very limited, and resources are scarce, let us seek another reality, an alternative vision, one which begins with the praises of the heavenly host, moves on to the praises of the prophets, apostles, martyrs and saints of the church, and ends with ourselves. It is as if we let these others pray and sing for us: we need to feel their presence, to hear their pain caught up in praise, and this is what this chapel allows us to do. This is how we can discover the secret of that 'blessedness' in suffering, the secret which all the Beatitudes seek to convey – an experience of God who enters into our pain yet also transcends it. So it begins with a prayer of lament at our human condition; but it ends with a hymn of praise to the God, Father, Son and Holy Ghost. May we learn this mystery of prayer for ourselves.

Appendix
Daniel 7:9–14

[9] As I watched, thrones were set in place, and an Ancient One took his throne, his clothing was white as snow, and the hair of his head like pure wool; his throne was fiery flames, and its wheels were burning fire. [10] A stream of fire issued and flowed out from his presence. A thousand thousands served him, and ten thousand times ten thousand stood attending him. The court sat in judgment, and the books were opened. [11] I watched then because of the noise of the arrogant words that the horn was speaking. And as I watched, the beast was put to death, and its body destroyed and given over to be burned with fire. [12] As for the rest of the beasts, their dominion was taken away, but their lives were prolonged for a season and a time.

Even the mosaic floor gives praise to God: the saints of the Western Church, represented before the Altar.

[13] As I watched in the night visions, I saw one like a human being coming with the clouds of heaven. And he came to the Ancient One and was presented before him. [14] To him was given dominion and glory and kingship, that all peoples, nations, and languages should serve him. His dominion is an everlasting dominion that shall not pass away, and his kingship is one that shall never be destroyed.

Revelation 4:1–11

[1] After this I looked, and there in heaven a door stood open! And the first voice, which I had heard speaking to me like a trumpet, said, 'Come up here, and I will show you what must take place after this.' [2] At once I was in the spirit, and there in heaven stood a throne, with one seated on the throne! [3] And the one seated there looks like jasper and carnelian, and around the throne is a rainbow that looks like an emerald. [4] Around the throne are twenty-four thrones, and seated on the thrones are twenty-four elders, dressed in white robes, with golden crowns on their heads. [5] Coming from the throne are flashes of lightning, and rumblings and peals of thunder, and in front of the throne burn seven flaming torches, which are the seven spirits of God; [6] and in front of the throne there is something like a sea of glass, like crystal. Around the throne, and on each side of the throne, are four living creatures, full of eyes in front and behind: [7] the first living creature like a lion, the second living creature like an ox, the third living creature with a face like a human face, and the fourth

living creature like a flying eagle. [8] And the four living creatures, each of them with six wings, are full of eyes all around and inside. Day and night without ceasing they sing, 'Holy, holy, holy, the Lord God the Almighty, who was and is and is to come.' [9] And whenever the living creatures give glory and honor and thanks to the one who is seated on the throne, who lives forever and ever, [10] the twenty-four elders fall before the one who is seated on the throne and worship the one who lives forever and ever; they cast their crowns before the throne, singing, [11] 'You are worthy, our Lord and God, to receive glory and honor and power, for you created all things, and by your will they existed and were created.'

The Te Deum (Book of Common Prayer)

We praise thee, O God : we acknowledge thee to be the Lord.
All the earth doth worship thee : the Father everlasting.
To thee all Angels cry aloud : the Heavens, and all the Powers therein.
To thee Cherubim and Seraphim : continually do cry,
Holy, Holy, Holy : Lord God of Sabaoth;
Heaven and earth are full of the Majesty : of thy glory.
The glorious company of the Apostles : praise thee.
The goodly fellowship of the Prophets : praise thee.
The noble army of Martyrs : praise thee.
The holy Church throughout all the world : doth acknowledge thee;
The Father : of an infinite Majesty;
Thine honourable, true : and only Son;
Also the Holy Ghost : the Comforter.

Thou art the King of Glory : O Christ.
Thou art the everlasting Son : of the Father.
When thou tookest upon thee to deliver man : thou didst not abhor the Virgin's womb.
When thou hadst overcome the sharpness of death : thou didst open the Kingdom of Heaven to all believers.
Thou sittest at the right hand of God : in the glory of the Father.
We believe that thou shalt come : to be our Judge.
We therefore pray thee, help thy servants : whom thou hast redeemed with thy precious blood.
Make them to be numbered with thy Saints : in glory everlasting.

O Lord, save thy people : and bless thine heritage.
Govern them : and lift them up for ever.
Day by day : we magnify thee;
And we worship thy Name : ever world without end.
Vouchsafe, O Lord : to keep us this day without sin.
O Lord, have mercy upon us : have mercy upon us.
O Lord, let thy mercy lighten upon us : as our trust is in thee.
O Lord, in thee have I trusted : let me never be confounded.

Index